THE
CHANGING WEST

AND OTHER ESSAYS

BY

LAURENCE M. LARSON

PROFESSOR OF HISTORY IN THE
UNIVERSITY OF ILLINOIS

NORTHFIELD, MINNESOTA
NORWEGIAN-AMERICAN HISTORICAL ASSOCIATION
1937

PREFACE

The eight essays that comprise this volume are built upon a foundation of research and patient scholarship. The author's deepest concern, however, is not for the massing up of facts, but rather for appraisal and interpretation. The general field is American social and cultural history, but Professor Larson looks especially at the West and the Northwest, and in most of these essays he explores the domain of Norwegian-American life and activity.

The title essay lays emphasis upon fundamental processes of transition at work in modern America. With this study as a background, the author turns to the story of the Norwegians in the United States. He knows that story as a result not merely of a searching study of sources, printed and unprinted, but also of a lifetime of observation, beginning with a boyhood in a typical midwestern Norwegian frontier community. And yet it is not so much the story itself as the underlying motives and significant tendencies that engage his interest. He is aware of the fact that more than eleven decades have passed since the little sloop "Restaurationen" brought to American shores the first shipload of nineteenth-century Norwegian immigrants, and he takes advantage of a long perspective both in the themes that he selects and in the questions that he raises.

Some frontier scenes are described. Few readers will forget the author's vivid picture of a Norwegian-Irish feud in a pioneer Iowa community. But alongside that picture is a probing analysis of Norwegian contributions to American scholarship. Professor Larson is deeply interested in the intellectual and broadly cultural aspects of the adjustment of an immigrant people to the New World. This explains his study of the beginnings of Norwegian-American fiction, for example, and his appraisal of the contributions made by the distinguished scholar and novelist, Hjalmar Hjorth Boyesen. It explains similarly his sympathetic description of the role of the lay preacher in the life of the pioneer Norwegian settlements and his fascinating account of the immigrants in relation to the "Yankee school." In dealing with particular aspects of a big story, he does not forget his general setting, and so he offers a comprehensive survey of the part played by Norwegians in the history of the Northwest.

I trust that Professor Larson will permit me to add that his friends and associates desired to bring out this book in honor of his election to the vice presidency, and his forthcoming elevation to the presidency, of the American Historical Association. When, about a year and a half ago, I ventured to suggest to him the idea of bringing together in book form some of his essays, I was well aware of the fact that his previously published works were mainly in the field of English and early Norse history, but I also knew of his deep interest in the story of the Norwegians in America, and I expressed the hope that he would focus his attention upon that subject. He took kindly to the suggestion and the result is the present volume. The Norwegian-American Historical Association feels honored in being permitted to sponsor the book, and in doing so it offers its congratulations to Professor Larson not only upon the high distinction that has come to him at the hands of the national historical organization but also upon the many and important contributions that he has made to American historiography.

THEODORE C. BLEGEN

THE UNIVERSITY OF MINNESOTA
MINNEAPOLIS

CONTENTS

ILLUSTRATIONS

THE CHANGING WEST
AND OTHER ESSAYS

PUBLISHER'S NOTE

Professor Larson's essays on "Hjalmar Hjorth Boyesen," "Scandinaven, Professor Anderson, and the Yankee School," and "The Lay Preacher in Pioneer Times" have not previously appeared in print. The other essays in this volume have been published elsewhere, but have been revised by the author for inclusion in this collection. "The Changing West" was prepared originally as an address given before the Illinois State Historical Society on December 2, 1924, and was published in the *Journal* of that institution for January, 1925. "The Norwegian Element in the Northwest" was read before the Mississippi Valley Historical Association at a meeting in Urbana, Illinois, in December, 1933, and was published in the *American Historical Review* for October, 1934. For permission to reprint these papers the author and the Norwegian-American Historical Association desire to express their thanks to the editors of the two periodicals mentioned. "The Norwegian Element in the Field of American Scholarship" is based upon an address delivered at the Norwegian Centennial Celebration in Minneapolis in 1925, and is here reprinted, with considerable revision and with a change in title, from volume 2 of the Norwegian-American Historical Association's series of *Studies and Records*. The essay on "The Convention Riot at Benson Grove, Iowa, in 1876" was first published in volume 6 of the same series, and the study of "Tellef Grundysen and the Beginnings of Norwegian-American Fiction" appeared in volume 8.

On the third day of December in the year 1818 President Monroe affixed his signature to a resolution of the two houses of Congress creating a new state in what was then almost the farthest west. A new commonwealth, the third to be organized in what was earlier known as the Northwest Territory, was by this act admitted into the expanding union of American states. The recognition of this particular region as worthy of statehood may be regarded as one of the major events in American history; for the fates had decreed that this youthful group of frontier settlements was to have a brilliant future, that in wealth and power and influence Illinois was to outstrip all her sisters among the newer states.

At the same time one must recognize the fact that the history of Illinois did not begin with the act of admission to the federal union. Before there was a state there was a territory, and still earlier there was a large undefined area called the Illinois country. Long before the American pioneer had begun to organize communities on the river banks of Illinois, soldiers and traders, farmers and missionaries had come into the land to occupy it and to hold it for the greater glory of the king of France. More than two hundred and fifty years have passed since the first white man (presumably some unknown French trader) wandered across the prairies of Illinois. During that long lapse of time much has happened in the great commonwealth, much that has been important not only for the state itself but for the nation and for all the western world.

It is not the purpose of this discussion, however, to deal specifically with the subject of Illinois. The plan is rather to present a few general facts relating to the greater area which includes Illinois and which we usually call the West. But the term " West " is not necessarily limited to geographical facts, nor does it need to mean a definite area. For America has a human as well as a physical map, and it is the West as it appears on the human map to which the writer wishes to direct his attention.

If one goes back to an earlier generation he will find that the most reliable and the most widely read historians had no profound interest in the great human movements that have made the West what it now is. These movements were not ignored, but they were not studied with the care that was given to older themes. Bancroft and Parkman, Bryant and Hildreth, Palfrey, Higginson, and Justin Winsor, Frothingham, Schouler, Henry Adams, and Emma Willard, these were all of New England ancestry and born in the good state of Massachusetts. With two or possibly three exceptions, they all had academic degrees from Harvard College. They were, therefore, thoroughly grounded in the New England tradition, a virile and quite persistent tradition. They were consequently not disposed to underrate the achievements of the Puritan colonies. Writing from the viewpoint of their own commonwealth, it was only natural that they should give much attention to the development of Puritan ideals and to the abiding influence of New England leadership. It would be idle to deny that this viewpoint is to a large extent entirely correct; at the same time it is also true that modern America is the product of many influences and has drawn strength and wisdom from many sources.

The difficulty with the theories of the older school was that they did not adequately interpret the forces that were shaping and reshaping American society in the nineteenth century. For it is a far cry from the ideals of the seaboard in the seventeenth century to those that dominate life in the West in the twentieth. Our social and institutional systems have changed, radically and profoundly; but why have they changed?

In the earlier years of the nineties a young historian at

the University of Wisconsin was maturing a new interpretation of American development. At a meeting of the American Historical Association held in Chicago in 1893 a paper was presented by Professor Frederick Jackson Turner on "The Significance of the Frontier in American History." In this paper the author argued that "the true point of view in the history of this nation is not the Atlantic coast, it is the great West." The fundamental institutions of the Republic had, indeed, been developed within a limited area on the Atlantic seaboard; but as the nation expanded into the vast unoccupied spaces of the West, these institutions had to be re-established again and again, and usually had to be adapted to the conditions of a new environment. "This perennial rebirth, this fluidity of American life, this expansion westward with its new opportunities, its continuous touch with the simplicity of primitive society, furnish the forces dominating American character."

Rarely has a new doctrine in the field of history found such ready acceptance. Theodore Roosevelt, who was working at the time on his *Winning of the West*, was one of the first to feel the force of Professor Turner's contention. Justin Winsor shows clearly the influence of the new interpretation in his *Westward Movement*, which was published in 1897. In the course of a decade there had arisen a new school of historical thinkers, all actively studying American history from the western point of view. If the historical profession in America has its prophets Professor Turner belongs to the major group.

But where was this West? And what was the American frontier? At first the West was just back of the seaboard, just beyond the settlements. The earliest villages in the Connecticut Valley were "out west." The area covered by the tide of settlement steadily advancing across the apparently boundless stretches was the West. But, looked at from another angle, it may be defined as a peculiar condition of social life, the sort of life that frequently develops when men and women who are more or less controlled by the instincts of civilization seek to establish homes in the wilderness. And the frontier, to quote Professor Turner once more, is " the outer edge of the wave of settlement, the meeting point between savagery and civilization."

The West that has most profoundly affected American life is the great plain lying just beyond the Appalachian highlands toward the setting sun. It is the wonderful valley of the Mississippi with all that belongs to it as far west as the hundredth meridian. This vast expanse of forest and prairie, one thousand miles from east to west and more than a thousand from north to south, is the most richly endowed area of large dimensions in all the earth. Regions may be found in other countries where the soil is more fertile, where the mineral wealth is greater, or where certain other resources are more abundant; but on no other continent has Providence arranged such a remarkable combination of soil fertility, of coal and iron, of favorable location, climate, and rainfall as the pioneers found in the American West. And there it all lay one hundred and fifty years ago, seemingly boundless and almost untouched, a field for human energy that had no rival.

When the Revolution closed, some of the possibilities of the western country had become known to the frontiersmen, but scarcely more than known. Such settlements as had actually been formed beyond the mountains served merely to emphasize the primeval conditions. But great forces were already mustering to invade and to conquer this enticing land. All along the frontier the pioneers were gathering, all eager for the great adventure. Soon they were pouring through the mountain gaps, crossing the portages, or drifting down the watercourses, and finally finding their places in a long, thin line of toiling humanity, facing the overpowering forces of the wilderness, but facing them without fear.

The host that conquered the West was a highly composite body, but it was overwhelmingly American. Among the pioneers were men and women from New England and from other parts of the seaboard, nearly all of whom were of English and Welsh ancestry. There was also a sprinkling of French Huguenots and a few Dutch from the towns on the Hudson. From the broad valleys of Pennsylvania and Virginia came Germans, often called the Pennsylvania Dutch, who were as yet scarcely Americanized, though nearly all were of American birth. But the most aggressive and the most prominent leaders appear to have been among the Scotch-Irish who were mustering in the valleys farther to the west.

Among the many elements that combined to mold American life, three were outstanding: the Puritan of New England, the Cavalier of the South, and the Scotch-Irish of the frontier. Each of these had its own peculiar outlook and its own peculiar mission. There was courteous, refined life in the mansions of the southern estates. New England, realizing the value of intellectual leadership, fostered education and emphasized the things that belong to the spirit. But of these things there was little in the wretched cabins of the Allegheny valleys. The Scotch-Irishman was poor, he was a stranger to display and ceremony, he had little enthusiasm for books. And yet, there are those who believe that the typical American of those days was not the Puritan of the East, but the later Puritan of the frontier, the grim trader, farmer, and fighter, whose ancestors came from Ulster.

The Scotch-Irishmen were not Irish as to race: they were the descendants of Scotch and English colonists who had been settled in northern Ireland early in the seventeenth century. Many of these had come from the Scottish border where raids and feuds and petty warfare had been the rule for generations. When they settled in Ireland they neither found peace nor brought peace, and a new border was formed. After a hundred years these new Ulstermen began to emigrate in large numbers; they found homes in America on the very edge of the settled area where the red man was

tracing the boundary in American blood. The Scotch-Irishman made a very effective frontiersman; and the long-limbed
pioneer with the long knife, the long gun, and the long
memory soon put the fear of the Lord into the skulking
tribesmen.

But whatever his ancestry, German or British, the western
pioneer was a remarkable man. Living under conditions
that usually allowed the healthy alone to survive infancy,
his was a strong and virile race. Though coarse, ill-bred,
and often unlettered, he knew the varied life of the mountain and the forest, and that, too, was knowledge. In a
simple way he was resourceful, for he knew how to deal
with the recurring crises of his environment; and he was
nearly always able to provide for the needs of his family
from the scanty storehouse of the wilderness. He was often
of a restless mood and easily dissatisfied with his new home.
But by nature the pioneer was hopeful and strong of heart,
though he usually sought to realize his hopes in new and
supposedly better localities. He wandered widely and often
aimlessly, but the nation grew as he wandered.

It is not so easy to generalize about the westward
movement, for after all it produced a great variety of types
and social units. Wisconsin did not develop like the Gulf
coast, nor was early Arkansas very much like the Western
Reserve. There were, however, three facts that characterized the entire movement: it was American; it was democratic; it was Protestant.

The movement was American not only because the pioneers were commonly of native birth, but also because they
usually had no interests beyond their own country. Such
connections with Europe as some had tried to keep intact
in the older homes could be maintained only with great
difficulty in the newer settlements. Such interest as they
may have had in European affairs was soon engulfed in the
duties and the troubles of a new environment. As the line
of settlement advanced, the influence of the Old World was

constantly diminishing. The thoughts that stirred in the mind of the frontiersman were largely the product of the western soil.

It was a democratic movement. The pioneer host was unique in this, that it recognized equality not only as a theory but as a fact. In the strenuous battle with untamed nature, a battle that raged on a front of more than a thousand miles, privilege could not flourish and there could be no leisure class. The frontier did, indeed, always respect the authority of leadership; but it was a leadership based on recognized strength and achievement. In the new social order ancestry was not highly regarded and genealogies were not known.

It was a Protestant movement. Far to the front on the skirmish line rode the Methodist preacher and the Presbyterian elder, industriously gathering their adherents into societies and churches. The Baptist minister and the Congregational missionary were not far behind, the one finding an unusually fertile field in the South, the other achieving a greater success in the North. The Lutheran, the Anglican, the Quaker, the Mennonite, and the Catholic, with many other types of believers, were all represented in the new settlements. Soon came Alexander Campbell heading a new religious movement, the Church of Christ, a typical product of western democracy. Thus there was a great variety of religions in the Old West, but the vast majority of the pioneers were Protestants, and many of their leaders were men who had drunk deep from the springs of Calvinism. And the Calvinist believes in simplicity and emphasizes the essential equality of human souls.

The making of a western community has been described in masterly fashion by Herbert Quick in his novel, *Vandemark's Folly*. As a work of literary art Quick's novel may be rather ordinary; but as a human document it has the virtue of truthful realism. It is the story of the covered wagon bearing westward across the prairies of Iowa its precious burden of commonplace humanity, men and women who were generally admirable, though not always good and wise and strong, and other men and women whose souls had been darkened with evil, though they were never wholly without strength and goodness. Of such the West was formed.

It has been my privilege to see the prairies of Iowa stretching out toward the hazy horizon with only the gently rolling hills to break the monotony of the view. Here and there we could see at times a covered wagon, or two, or three, or a dozen, headed courageously toward the promised land. Soon there were human beings living in dugouts, in sod shanties, or in the more palatial log houses. I have seen the slow ox teams pulling the plow through the tough sod. I have heard the untutored preachers of pioneer days shouting condemnation on a little impoverished world which seemed to them to be wholly lost in the sins of pride and arrogance and vanity! And I have shared the emotions of toilers as they watched the coming of the railway which was to put an end to pioneer conditions. This was pioneer life in its last stage. It was a relatively brief stage but it was real while it lasted.

There was, however, a great difference between the community that my family helped to build and the settlements of the older West. The New England Puritan was discreetly absent and there was no Scotch-Irishman in sight. The Methodist clergyman was hovering around the edges but made only the slightest impression. The English language was rarely heard; where it was used away from the public school grounds it was employed chiefly for the purposes of trade and baseball. For ours was a community of immigrants from the isles and the valleys of northern Europe. They had all suffered hard conditions in their own country; they had found even more severe hardships in the New World. But the promise of the West was great and every heart was hopeful. They were hardy men and strong women with honest purposes and willing hands. Their minds were heavy but intelligent and they sought honestly for the boundaries between right and wrong. They had a deep reverence for religious truth, but they worshiped the Lord in a foreign tongue. Such intellectual food as they seemed to need they found in sermons, in books, and in newspapers in their own language. They knew very little about the American constitution but they rarely failed to vote. They were the salt of the earth, but they were not Americans.

The West was changing — the entire nation was changing. The changes were due in great part to the efforts of an energetic people in a rich territory; in part to the introduction of new elements into our population. Great cities had been built, among them the city of Chicago, rising in magnificent power from the swamps on the shore of Lake Michigan. Railways radiating in all directions were gathering the wealth of an empire into the warehouses of that city or distributing the surplus to other parts of the land. Chicago may serve as a convenient symbol of the transformation that has come to the inland plain. For it illustrates all the changes that have occurred since the simple days of Boone and Cartwright and Davy Crockett.

But when we study the progress of American settlement in the last hundred years, the most significant fact that we note is the appearance of certain great alien groups, especially after the year 1850. There has probably not been a time when there was no migration to the American colonies or to the American republic; but earlier movements of this sort can hardly compare with those that began in the first half of the nineteenth century. Since that time there has been a steady and powerful stream of immigrants coming from every country in Europe and coming continuously till the current was checked by the Great War and by recent legislation. Irish, Germans, and Scandinavians were among the earliest to arrive in large numbers; but soon came Slavs and Latins, Jews and Greeks. For some time the immigrants continued the traditions of the older pioneers and went out into the unoccupied areas to build homes on the free land; later, as the country became industrialized, they found employment in mines and factories. Thus the foreigner has promoted American development to an extent that is simply enormous, at least on the material side.

Today the alien element in the United States comprises nearly a third of the entire population. In the West and Northwest the percentage is even greater than for the country at large; for the immigrant population is massed north of Mason and Dixon's Line. This means that in the country as a whole there are thirty to thirty-five million men and women who were born abroad or who have at least one parent of alien birth. A little more than one-half of the white population is counted as native American, but this does not always imply colonial ancestry, for millions of those who are rated as natives have grandparents of foreign birth.

The census of 1920 found approximately 2,300,000 persons who were born in Germany or German Austria. Of native Italians, 1,600,000 were found; and almost as many were credited to Russia, most of whom were no doubt of Hebrew blood. The Poles, the Scandinavians, the Irish, and the natives of Great Britain were approximately of the same number, each counting something more than a million. Many other nationalities appear in the census but in smaller numbers, Hungary leading among the lesser groups with 400,000. The states with the largest percentage of inhabitants who are still classified as aliens are Wisconsin, Minnesota, and North Dakota, the figures running from sixty to sixty-eight. In South Dakota, Montana, Illinois, and Michigan the percentage ranges from fifty to fifty-five.

If these figures have any meaning it must be that great ethnic changes are in progress throughout the entire nation. It is quite clear that the future race in America will be not English or even British, but European. And it may be that various regions will develop separate and various types. As one studies the human map of America one seems to find three great areas, each with a different situation and a different problem. The South is still American in the older sense, its white population being almost entirely descended from colonial ancestry. In the group of states that center about New York there is racial chaos. Irishmen, Italians, Jews, Englishmen, and Germans have settled in that area in large groups but most of them have come in relatively recent times and the process of assimilation, a difficult process in the circumstances, has hardly begun.

The third area is that which covers the upper stretches of the Middle West. If one should draw a line from Detroit to St. Louis and continue it westward to the hundredth meridian one would approximate the southern boundary of a great region, including the whole, or the greater part, of ten states, all of which are inhabited to a large extent by alien elements. This region still contains an important native American element, which in some states continues to be the dominating element. It is dominating first of all because it holds in its possession the rare treasures of American culture and the great traditions of the American past. Again, it is able to dominate because the various alien groups are rarely able to present a united front in the contest for power. But the old colonial stock is obviously shrinking, and in some quarters it is being slowly absorbed into the newer population.

This situation, though somewhat alarming at first sight, is, however, no cause for despair. On the whole, the racial situation in this part of the country is more satisfactory than in any other large section in the entire North. For it happens that the larger elements in the population are closely related in race and in history. They have all come from central and northwestern Europe, from Germany, Scandinavia, the Netherlands, and the British Isles. Excepting the Irish, these are all of Germanic stock and are simply varieties of the same racial type. And the Irish, through their long connection with Great Britain, have learned the English language and have accepted the principles of Germanic civilization. The future race in the West, like the English of today, will be fundamentally Germanic. There are indeed many other nationalistic groups that have found permanent homes in this section, but these are scarcely of sufficient strength to affect the outcome.

The alien is here by invitation, even by urgent invitation. He once heard a distressful cry, " Come over and help us! " and he came. In the course of time he has profited much from his new environment; but he has paid in full for everything that he has received. On the farm, in the mine, on the railway line, on the street, and in the skyscraper he has lifted the heavy burdens and has carried the heavy load.

It would be folly to deny, however, that immigration has produced a real problem. For the foreigner has developed a consciousness that is somewhat disconcerting. He is organizing his forces and on occasion he is likely to make nationalistic demands. One needs only recall the stir made by certain groups in 1915 and 1916 to realize the possible danger from alien enthusiasts organized for political ends.

But here again the leaders of the Republic have been at fault. Having sown the wind, they now complain of the harvest. Time and again our political chieftains have appealed to the various alien elements to vote as a unit. Perhaps no one is more responsible for racial solidarity among the foreigners than the late Mark Hanna. In the campaign of 1896 he organized these groups wherever possible. In the political processions of that campaign German-Americans, Hebrew-Americans, Swedish-Americans, and other varities of alien-Americans marched under their separate nationalistic banners. Hanna is, it is true, only one of the many who have sinned in this respect, but it seems clear that of all the political generals who have dealt with the alien vote, he was the most effective and the most successful.

The significant fact is that through methods of this sort the foreign voters have become conscious of their strength. In some of the northwestern states they are now competing successfully for power with the native classes. In the state elections of the present year (1924), governors of Norwegian ancestry have been chosen in the states of Minnesota, North Dakota, and Montana. In the congress that convenes this week, Wisconsin, Minnesota, and the two Dakotas are represented by five senators of Scandinavian birth or blood. It is clear that the Northwest at least is no longer American in the older sense.

Political power rarely comes to the immigrant family before the second generation. There is much to learn and the alien learns it slowly. Unless he comes from a home in the British Isles he is fatally handicapped by his inability to use the language of the land. Meanwhile, he is building churches, organizing parochial schools, and founding theological seminaries. Sometimes he even builds a theater or begins to publish a newspaper in a foreign tongue. In all this his purpose is to perpetuate on American soil the particular language, creed, and culture that he has brought with him from the mother country. And for this he must not be condemned; for he, too, has an intellectual life which must be maintained, or the new citizen will be of little value to the land.

It has been stated above that the West was Protestant; it is still Protestant in large part, but its Protestantism is of a different type. The strongest single Protestant communion in Wisconsin, Minnesota, and the two Dakotas is the Lutheran church. In Illinois, Michigan, Iowa, and Nebraska, Lutheranism is second only to Methodism among the Protestant faiths. The strength of the Lutheran churches being relatively recent in the West, the influence of the Lutheran spirit, which is vitally different from that of Calvinism, has not yet begun to be felt so widely or so profoundly as numbers would seem to promise. But it is an influence with which the future will be forced to reckon.

In all these states and in many others the strongest church is not any one of the Protestant denominations but the great Roman Catholic church, which is today the most potent single moral force in that part of our country that we generally call the North.

These facts are not presented in the spirit of criticism: they are important parts of the evidence on which I base the argument that the West is changing — changing in racial type, in intellectual interest, in outlook, in religion, and in moral standards. The West that was is passing into history; the new West is still in the future.

The time will come when nearly all of the various elements that claim the American title will be fused into new racial units. The time will come when the bonds that bind so many of us to hearths and homes in other lands will lose their strength and the men with foreign ancestry will think of themselves as Americans only. When that time comes the process that we call Americanization will have been completed. It may be seriously doubted, however, whether the process has gone forward at a normal rate of progress during the past decade; on the contrary it seems that one may safely affirm that in this year of our Lord, 1924, the Republic has drifted farther away from the ancient ideal of a unified nation than at any other time since the Civil War.

Americanization, like all the processes of history, is a slow process and cannot be hastened beyond a normal rate. Men have never become loyal Americans through compulsion. To be a real citizen one must not only acknowledge an outward allegiance to the symbols of the state; one must accept as his own personal possession the principles and the ideals that form the framework of our national culture. And this is a thing of the spirit.

It is easy to retard the process. In our own West today

we see race rising against race, church arrayed against church. Where patience and toleration were once the rule there is anger and bitterness, rancor and fear.[1] But upon such foundations the more perfect nationality to which all patriotic citizens look forward cannot be built.

Fortunately the voice of experience tells us that this condition of subversive discord is not likely to have a long career. The history of the American people is emphatic in its assurance that movements of a Know-nothing character cannot flourish on western soil. The common sense of American citizenship is sure to assert its authority and constructive labor will be resumed.

The discussion has wandered far away from the point at which it began. But it is also a far cry from the French fathers to the grand cyclops. Moreover, the subject is a changing subject, for this has always been a changing West.

[1] It is to be noted that this address was prepared and delivered in 1924 when the Ku Klux Klan was at the height of its influence and power.

One hundred and two years ago a small group of Norwegian immigrants straggled into northern Illinois and began to establish a frontier community in the valley of the Fox River. They were the advance party of a mighty host which for nearly a century has been pouring its strength into the great Northwest. The little Fox River settlement was doubtless very much like any other pioneer community, but it had a unique importance. It was the beginning of a new Norwegian colonial movement, which in the course of two generations helped to push the boundaries of settlement northward and westward from the Great Lakes to the upper Missouri. There the movement was checked for a time by the broad stretches of the arid lands; but it soon broke through the barrier and continued the process of expansion to the shores of Puget Sound.

The history of this movement is a chapter in the wonderful story of the American pioneer, a race of sturdy adventurers with strong hands and strong souls, who conquered and built the American West. The life of the frontiersman is a fascinating theme, but it is one with which this paper is not concerned. The task assigned in this instance is far less romantic: it is to bring a measure of tribute to another class of pioneers — to the men and women of Norwegian blood who have devoted their energies to the cause of learning, who have sought and found careers in the field of intellectual achievement.

In a certain sense the scholar is nearly always a pioneer. Whether he toils in the quiet atmosphere of archives or laboratories, or seeks to penetrate the mysteries of life as it unfolds itself in the great outdoors, his work is essentially pioneering. The scholar loves to travel on the advancing frontiers of truth. His delight is to explore the wonders of a new land. He finds his happiness in breaking new ground, in tilling new soil. For his is a great calling: to him is given the duty of maintaining and extending the boundaries of the many kingdoms that belong to the human mind.

In the summer of 1925 American citizens of Norwegian birth or ancestry gathered in sundry places to take proper note of the fact that a full century had passed since the first shipload of Norwegian emigrants had sailed forth to build new homes in the western world. On these occasions a prominent question was always this: What have we Americans of the Norwegian race accomplished in these hundred years? The answer to this question can be found in many places, perhaps most conveniently in Norlie's encyclopedic *History of the Norwegian People in America,* a product of the enthusiasm of the centennial year. No doubt one could continue to write in more detail of what success our people have attained in business, in politics, in art, in the field of religion, or even in professional life; but these subjects lie without the limits of the present survey. There is, however, a series of questions that are not so frequently asked and have never been adequately answered; to these the writer wishes to address himself. What have we achieved in the field of American scholarship? What share have we had in the promotion of knowledge? What important discoveries have we made and published? What recognition have we received in the guilds of scientific thought?

When one belongs to a people who take pride in blunt frankness and honesty of speech, one cannot avoid replying to these questions that we have not yet won the recognition for scientific achievement that seemingly should be ours. The Norwegian element in the New World is not without prominent scholars and brilliant men; but the number of those who have attained a wider fame in the republic of science is not yet appreciably great. Having said this, one should hasten to add, however, that this state of affairs is

exactly what one would expect to find. It must not be for-
gotten that the Norwegian-Americans, as an immigrant people, have had all the handicaps of an alien folk. Nevertheless,
it can be safely affirmed that among the so-called alien
groups, excepting only such as have come from lands where
English is spoken, the Norwegian element stands well to the
front in almost every field of national life. Until we have
become completely adjusted to the intellectual environment
within which we move, we cannot, of course, expect to com-
pete with the native element on equal terms. But the Norse
virtue of persistence has begun to show results. A splendid
body of young citizens bearing Norwegian names is actively
engaged in the pursuit of learning in all the great universities
throughout the land, and the years to come are full of
promise.

One often wonders why Norwegian intellect has come so
late into the competition; but the reason is, after all, easily
found. It must first be remembered that one hundred years
ago the Norwegian nation was not homogeneous either in
race or in culture. The rural element was still Norwegian
like the very soil itself, while those who lived in the cities
were largely of a mixed race. Names like Grieg, Michelet,
Obstfelder, Christie, and Konow, to list a few only, testify to
origins that were not Norwegian nor even Scandinavian. In
the course of the nineteenth century these two elements were
fused into a fairly homogeneous nationality; that process
had scarcely begun, however, when the sloop folk set out to
sea. To a large extent the new Norway of the great West
has drawn its population from the farming class. The Norwegian farmers were not without culture, but their culture
was that of the countryside.

Through all its history the rural class had loved the land:
the soil gave home and sustenance and sometimes even
wealth; but it also gave the owner his name and his social
position. Now the immigrants had come to a country where
farms could be had almost for the asking. Thus they natu-

rally followed the advance of rural settlement over the beckoning prairies of the free land. It was only when the supply of good free land had been exhausted that the children of the pioneer began to make large use of educational opportunities. Meanwhile they were helping to build an empire in the New World. To this work they contributed thought and energy and active leadership, but their efforts were chiefly directed toward material ends. Wrestling with nature and struggling with poverty, they found little time or strength to spare for study, and they saw little value in any form of knowledge that was not directly related to their personal tasks or duties as farmers and citizens.

It is important to observe also that such intellectual interest as the Norwegian pioneer did possess was centered largely in the church. He recognized but one distinctly honorable profession, that of the Lutheran ministry; his chief joy was to listen to the preaching of a gifted son. There was, of course, the law; but to the Norwegian farmer's mind the lawyer was usually an educated trickster who found much profit and took keen pleasure in foreclosing mortgages and prosecuting unfortunate debtors. Nevertheless, a relatively large number of young Norwegians have entered the legal profession and have shared in its rewards, though the number of those who have risen to eminence is not great.

For some time the northern immigrants found it necessary to recruit a corps of trained leaders in the mother country, but most of those who came to the settlements with university degrees belonged to the clerical profession. It is quite clear that many of these would, under more favorable circumstances, have developed into real scholars; however, the task of a clergyman in pioneer days and under frontier conditions was too arduous to allow him much rest from the common duties of a pastor's life.

Furthermore, such energies as could be spared the theologians on the frontier too often gave to religious controversy.

For more than fifty years there raged throughout the Norwegian settlements a series of conflicts that can be classified only as theological warfare. Almost the earliest memories of the writer are concerned with what was supposed to be religious discussion but was certainly not conceived in the spirit of holiness. One should scarcely need to argue that the things that belong to the intellectual life cannot flourish in an atmosphere of wrath. The contending parties did, indeed, establish higher schools; for a long time, however, these dragged out a pitiful existence, not only because their patrons were poor, but because their faculties were frequently torn with strife.

It is not particularly pleasant to dwell on these developments in the history of our people, but they must not be overlooked; they help to explain why the Norwegian competitor has come so tardily into the arena of American scholarship. There have always been some, however, who cherished the hope that some day all these warring factions would be fused into a single unity living at peace with itself and with the rest of the world. The time came when this thought began to be realized, and the cause of scholarship has profited greatly by the progressive union of Norwegian churches. By this union of effort it has become possible to enlarge, to rebuild, and to reorganize the Norwegian-American colleges so as to give them a wider usefulness, a greater efficiency, and higher possibilities for the training of young men and women.

Scholars are of many kinds; but for present purposes it may be sufficiently accurate to classify them under two heads; those who find their chief satisfaction in working with the knowledge already acquired by the race, and those whose ambitions prompt them to search for new knowledge where none has searched before. The former is the larger and in some respects the more influential group. It includes the great majority of those who give instruction in the higher schools. They are the men and the women to whom society has entrusted the treasures of civilization. Their special duty is not to enlarge the kingdom of knowledge but to maintain it and to keep its boundaries unimpaired. It is a great duty and a vital task.

While it is quite true that all teachers are not scholars, one finds in the teaching profession many of the choicest minds, grand souls who have drunk deep from Mimir's fount. Of such scholars our Norwegian citizenry had produced its full quota. We find them in schools and colleges, in educational institutions of every grade. Many have remained in the Northwest among their own people; many others have gone forth into other sections, and today men and women of Norwegian ancestry are giving instruction in nearly all the important colleges of the land.[1]

It would not be possible to list the names of even the outstanding men and women who belong in this group. But there is one name that the writer feels called upon to give prominent mention, the name of a man whose work as a teacher has been peculiarly important. It is the privilege of certain teachers to possess the gift of power and insight needed not only to instruct their classes but to inspire the individual student with faith in his chosen profession and to give him the sort of encouragement that youth so frequently needs. The writer has sat in the classroom of such a man; he has been allowed to share his knowledge, his faith, his enthusiasm; and he takes this opportunity to acknowledge a personal debt to Professor Julius E. Olson of the University of Wisconsin, who for nearly fifty years has kept the fires lit on the altar of Norsedom, thus gaining a primacy which all should be glad to acknowledge.

The scholars of the second group are less concerned with teaching; they find their chief interest in research. It should not be said that research is necessarily a higher function, for

[1] John A. Hofstead has listed nearly four hundred American universities, colleges, and other institutions of approximately college grade in which Norwegian men and women hold or have held teaching positions; *American Educators of Norwegian Origin*, 297–307 (Minneapolis, 1931).

one may be a scholar of the finest type without indulging the passion for scientific investigation. Nevertheless, research is of vital importance, for out of research comes progress. The Norwegian citizens of the great Republic who have won real distinction as productive scholars form a relatively small body; but among them are men who in their particular fields of learning have gained the recognition that comes only with the production of a masterpiece.

Scholarship of the productive type began to show its first signs of life among us in 1874, when Rasmus B. Anderson published his first book, *America Not Discovered by Columbus*. In the course of the following decade Anderson published a series of volumes, most of which dealt with subjects of interest to the reader of history, and all of which called for a certain measure of historical investigation. Anderson's work is distinctly of the pioneer type; it is not always critical and the author is sometimes too aggressive in stating the rights and the achievements of the Norwegian people. But his writings were, in their own day, of first rate importance, for they broke new ground and turned the thoughts of American investigators toward fields of which they had only the slightest knowledge.

There may be those who would affirm that the real pioneer in the realm of Norse-American culture was not the enthusiastic and somewhat belligerent citizen of Madison but the more refined and peaceful New Yorker, Hjalmar Hjorth Boyesen. Boyesen wrote his *Gunnar* before Anderson had finished his study of the Vinland voyages, but the two books came from the press in the same year. Moreover, *Gunnar* is a novel, and as literature is generally classed among the arts, it does not belong within the limits of this discussion.

Boyesen's contribution to scholarship in the more specific sense was very slight. His essays have the excellence of form which one would expect to find in the writings of a literary artist, but they do not always reveal either profound insight or penetration. Boyesen was at his best in literary criticism, especially in his studies in Scandinavian literature, which he dealt with in a sympathetic and understanding spirit at a time when many prominent critics were indifferent or even hostile. His right to honorable mention in a survey of this sort is derived, however, chiefly from the fact that in a tactful and thoroughly effective manner he directed the attention of the American public to the culture of the Northland and to its claims to serious study.

In 1876, two years after the publication of Anderson's and Boyesen's first books, the cause of scholarship received new impetus by the establishment of Johns Hopkins University in Baltimore. Graduate work had, indeed, been attempted elsewhere; in 1877 two students of Norwegian birth, Anton B. Sander and Magnus C. Ihlseng, received the degree of doctor of philosophy at Yale University. Dr. Sander's scholastic history was destined to be brief;[2] but Magnus Ihlseng entered immediately upon a long and fruitful career both in teaching and in research. He was still in academic work when he died in 1930.[3]

While the older colleges may, therefore, be allowed a certain measure of priority even in post-graduate work, it is generally agreed that organized graduate study in the United States really dates from the opening year of Johns Hopkins University. The founding of this new institution with its emphasis on individual study in seminars and laboratories almost led to a revolution in university work. Many other graduate schools were soon founded; and among the young men who entered upon advanced study in these institutions were several from the Norwegian settlements in the West. Very few of these earlier Norwegian scholars, however,

[2] Sander taught languages (Greek, Latin, Hebrew, and German) at Luther College during the academic year 1878–79. I do not know that he had a later appointment.

[3] Professor Ihlseng began his college teaching as instructor in physics at Columbia College. Later he held a professorship in the Colorado School of Mines, a deanship in Pennsylvania State College, the presidency of Blairsville College in Blairsville, Pennsylvania, and a professorship in the Polytechnic Institute of Brooklyn.

made any distinct impression on the learned guilds of the land. Too often they were forced to seek positions in the newer West, where facilities for serious research were uniformly poor. Albert E. Egge, whose training had prepared him for fruitful investigation along linguistic lines, ended his labors in the Agricultural College at Pullman, Washington. Agnes Mathilde Wergeland wasted her splendid talents on the desert airs of Wyoming. Andrew Fossum gave his energies to the service of his countrymen in the classrooms of St. Olaf College at a time when effective teaching was the only need to which the college authorities were able to give an adequate recognition. Olaus Dahl was called from Yale to a more promising environment at the University of Chicago; but death overtook him when his task was scarcely begun.

And so the nineteenth century closed without much promise. When Mr. A. N. Marquis, in 1899, began to publish *Who's Who in America,* he found only about a dozen Norwegians who had achieved something more than a mere provincial prominence. In the whole list there was only one man, Rasmus B. Anderson, who could qualify as a productive scholar. There were splendid names in the list, those of Storm Bull, the engineer, Georg Sverdrup, the intellectual chieftain of Augsburg Seminary, and Laur. Larsen, the venerable president of Luther College, all of whom might have become eminent in scholarship but had found their careers in more practical lines.

Times change, however, and sometimes they change for the better. The last twenty-five years have witnessed a tremendous advance in productive scholarship, and in this advance the children of the Norse immigrant have had their share. Sixty years ago the Norwegian pioneer had produced only two books that an American scholar might care to read. Today there is almost a library of books and pamphlets written by Norwegian-American authors in the English language. The output has, of course, taken a great variety of forms and the quality has not always been high; but among these new writers are men and women of real genius. In the field of the novel, for example, there are such outstanding authors as Martha Ostenso and O. E. Rølvaag.

Twelve years ago, when Mr. Marquis was preparing the thirteenth edition of *Who's Who,* he found at least 140 persons of Norwegian birth or blood who were worthy of mention in his publication. In the edition for 1934-35 the number has increased to about 190. This is a little more than three-fifths of one per cent of the entire number included in the volume. In view of the fact that the Norwegian element can scarcely comprise more than one, or at most one and one-half per cent of the entire population of the country, and that this group includes only two generations of native-born Norwegian-American citizens, this is an impressive showing.

The list in *Who's Who* is drawn from a variety of occupations — more than fifty when all are counted. It is interesting to observe that the clerical profession is perhaps still the most popular in the Norwegian settlements. Mr. Marquis has included sketches of twenty-five men who are actively engaged in pastoral work or as teachers in theological seminaries. If the clergymen who have entered other professional work, such as journalism or college teaching, were counted with these, the number would easily reach forty.

A strong competing body is that of the successful politicians, the men who have achieved election or appointment to high office in state or nation. Twenty-eight belong in this group, including fourteen present or past members of the national House of Representatives. Another distinctly secular group is composed of men who are concerned with business or business administration. Fourteen have qualified for leadership in these occupations; half of the group would be classed as corporation officials.

Of lawyers who have achieved something more than local eminence, Mr. Marquis has found eleven; five of these have seats on the judicial bench. The fine arts (music, painting, and sculpture) have eight representatives, among whom are such distinguished artists as Jonas Lie and F. Melius Christiansen. Eight men qualify as leaders in journalism. Medicine and surgery have seven places in the list; but the number signifies very little, for some of our choicest intellects are to be found in the medical profession. Engineering has at least three outstanding representatives, and the editor has included sketches of three men who wish to be known merely as authors.

The names that remain, a total of seventy-seven, are, with some exceptions, those of men and women who have made careers in colleges and universities. Of the academic professions the most popular seem to be education and the natural sciences, the numbers being respectively eighteen and twenty-four.[4] Sixteen are credited to the social sciences, five are concerned with language study, and four are occupied with the science of agriculture and the economics of the farm.

It is clear that no analysis of this sort can make any claims to even approximate accuracy. To begin with, nearly all the biographical directories are in a measure incomplete. In making up their lists of notables the editors have applied standards which are often quite arbitrary. In working through the materials as finally compiled one finds that there are careers, and many of them, that can easily be fitted into more than one category. There is also the difficulty that men of Norwegian ancestry cannot always be identified as such because of their somewhat Americanized surnames. All the same, these compilations, when used with discretion, cannot fail to be very enlightening; and a careful analysis of their contents will often be found highly suggestive.[5]

[4] Under the head of education I have grouped not only the men who give courses in the science and history of education, but also educational administrators (deans and presidents of teacher's colleges, liberal arts colleges, and universities).

[5] In the preparation of this paper the following compilations of the *Who's Who* type have been consulted: *American Educators of Norwegian Origin*, edited by John A. Hofstead (Minneapolis, 1931); *American Men of Science*, edited by

Scholarship of the productive type seems to flourish most naturally in the mild atmosphere of the university campus. The stronger academic institutions are provided with extensive libraries and laboratories, both of which are essential to productive work. One would naturally conclude that our academic citizenship would be found in greatest strength in the Northwest, where the Norwegian population is massed and is therefore able to exercise much influence in public affairs; such, however, is not the case. Some of the ablest representatives of Norwegian-American intellect are to be found in institutions that have no extensive Norwegian constituencies.

There is no desire to deny the obvious fact that strong men are finding places in the Norwegian-American colleges: men like Oscar L. Olson, who teaches English at Luther College; Julius Boraas, who occupies the chair of education at St. Olaf College; and P. M. Glasoe, who has long been professor of chemistry in the latter institution. Our most prolific scholar, Olaf Morgan Norlie, is also professor at Luther College. Norlie's classroom subject is psychology, but most of his energies are apparently devoted to the study and setting in order of historical and statistical materials relating directly and indirectly to the Norwegian churches in America. In this case the avocation is far more important (at least for the future) than the vocation. Dr. Norlie's work differs from that of nearly all of his fellow Norwegian scholars in that it is in large part written in the Norwegian language. Though his studies are extensive rather than intensive, their value and importance cannot be questioned.

There are also a fair number of our own men in responsible positions in the various state institutions in this section. At

J. M. Cattell and Jaques Cattell (New York, 1933); *Leaders in Education,* edited by J. M. Cattell (New York, 1932); *The School Calendar, 1824–1924,* compiled and edited by Olaf Morgan Norlie (Minneapolis, 1924); *Who's Who in America,* edited by A. N. Marquis (Chicago, 1934); *Who's Who in the Nation's Capitol,* edited by Stanley H. Williamson (Washington, [1934]); *Who's Who among North American Authors,* edited by Alberta Lawrence (Los Angeles, [1935]); *Who's Who among Pastors,* edited by O. M. Norlie (Minneapolis, 1928).

the University of Minnesota the Norwegian element has prominent representatives in several of the major departments.   Henry A. Erikson and William Anderson are in charge respectively of the work in physics and political science.   Botany and geology have outstanding members in Carl Otto Rosendahl and Frederick William Sardeson; the latter has also made important contributions to the science of paleontology.   Martin B. Ruud is winning fame as a penetrating student of English literature.   Oscar B. Jesness has written extensively on the problems of agricultural economics.   In the college of medicine there is Owen H. Wangensteen, who has contributed liberally to the literature of medical science.

Passing to the University of Wisconsin one should mention first of all two active men in the field of the humanities: Einar Haugen, who is in charge of the courses in Scandinavian languages, and Paul Knaplund, the chairman of the department of history, who has entered upon a highly promising career in English history.   On the scientific side are Conrad A. Elvehjem in agricultural chemistry, Olaf A. Hougen in chemical engineering, and James Johnson in horticulture, with a specialty in plant diseases.

Northwestern University has a scientist of high distinction in Oliver Justin Lee, who since 1929 has held the headship of the department of astronomy.   Ernest Oscar Melby is dean of the school of education on the Evanston campus. An earlier member of the faculty of this same institution was Arthur Andersen, who has become internationally known for his work in accountancy both on the theoretical and on the practical side.

Several Norwegian-Americans hold or have held important positions on the instructional or administrative forces of the University of Chicago.   Among these are J. C. M. Hanson, who for a long term served as associate director of libraries and as professor of library science, and F. W. H. Zachariasen, who has written extensively on the subject of physics. In Rush Medical College, Clark W. Finnerud gives courses in dermatology and Peter Bassoe has a professorship in clinical neurology. Olaf Bergeim lectures on physiological chemistry in the medical college of the University of Illinois.

At the University of Iowa Henning Larsen is building a reputation for fruitful research in Germanic philology. Two Norwegians hold important positions in Iowa State College at Ames: Julius A. Larsen in forestry and Irving E. Melhus in plant pathology.

Carl William Thompson is director of the school of commerce in the University of South Dakota. Mention should also be made of Dr. Edward Olson, who went to Vermillion as president in 1887 and thus achieved the distinction of being the first Norwegian to be elected to the presidency of a state university. President Olson's administration was brief; it was terminated by his untimely death two years later.[6] But in those years he initiated policies which, if they had been consistently pursued, would have done much to promote scholarship in the young university.

The number of scholars of Norwegian birth or descent who have found congenial employment in the great Northwest is naturally quite considerable; still, a survey of the entire field leads to the conclusion that some of the stronger examples of Norse intellect are to be found beyond the borders of the New Norway. Norwegian-American scholarship has long since burst the territorial bonds and has sent representatives forth into all the leading academic institutions in the land.

In the process of making such a survey one seems to note again a definite predilection for work in the natural sciences. Conrad Engerud Tharaldsen is professor of anatomy in New York Medical College in the city of New York. Herman L. Ibsen holds the chair of genetics in Kansas State

---

[6] President Olson was in the Tribune Building (Minneapolis) when it caught fire on November 30, 1889. His death was caused by a fall from a fire escape. He was then forty-two years old.

Agricultural College. Louis Helmar Jorstad of Washington University, St. Louis, has published a series of notable studies in bacteriology and related subjects. John P. Munson at the time of his death (1928) was giving courses in biology in the state normal school at Ellensburg, Washington. Arthur M. Johnson is professor of botany in the University of California at Los Angeles. Two men who have written extensively in the field of zoology are H. P. K. Agersborg, sometime professor of biology at James Millikin University, Decatur, Illinois, and Charles Eugene Johnson, head of the department of zoology in the State College of Forestry at Syracuse, New York.

Among those who cultivate the chemical sciences one should mention Arthur von Krogh Anderson of Pennsylvania State College, whose subject is physiological chemistry; Arnold H. Johnson at Montana State College, Bozeman; Arthur Knudson, who lectures on biological chemistry at Albany Medical College, Albany, New York; Sigfried M. Hauge, who is directing experimental work at Purdue University, Lafayette, Indiana; Gerhard Rollefson, who gives courses in the University of California at Berkeley; and John A. Widtsoe, sometime agricultural chemist in the University of Utah and for a period of five years the president of that institution.

In the field of mathematics prominent places are held by Nels G. Lennes at the University of Montana, John A. Eiesland at the University of West Virginia, and Oystein Ore at Yale. Arthur Ranum, the well known exponent of non-Euclidian geometry, held a chair in mathematics at Cornell University for nearly fifty years. One may continue the roll with the names of Trygve Yensen of the Westinghouse laboratories in East Pittsburgh, who has become widely known for his penetrating studies in metallurgy and electrical engineering; Oscar H. Reinholdt, who has held various positions with the federal government as mining engineer; M. L. Reymert of the Mooseheart Laboratory for Child Research at Mooseheart, Illinois, sometime professor of psychology at the University of Oslo; and the late John Koren, whose interest centered in sociological problems but who is best known for his work in statistics.

On the side of the older humanities the showing is quite satisfactory, though not so impressive as on that of the sciences. A prominent student and teacher of the classics was the late Andrew R. Anderson of Duke University, whose interest also extended to problems in the literary history of the northern peoples. Carl W. Blegen, sometime assistant director of the American School of Classical Studies in Athens, is professor of classical archaeology in the University of Cincinnati. In the field of English literature one finds two men of notable achievements: Louis J. Bredvold, who has recently been appointed head of the department of English at the University of Michigan, and Sigurd B. Hustvedt of the University of California at Los Angeles, whose studies in ballad literature have attracted wide and favorable attention.

The late Professor Theodore K. Urdahl taught economics in various places, last of all in the University of Southern California. Harry R. Tosdal teaches the same subject at Harvard. Among the devotees of the younger discipline of political science one notes the names of Arnold J. Lien of Washington University, St. Louis, and Clarence A. Berdahl of the University of Illinois, who has been honored by his fellow members of the American Political Science Association with several important offices in that organization.

In the membership of the ancient guild of historians there is now a respectable group of men and women who have achieved distinction in the subject of their choice. Of these it will be possible to name only a few. John O. Evjen, whose favorite subject is church history, has to his credit, among other publications, a remarkable study in Norwegian immigration into old New York chiefly in the days of the Dutch regime. N. A. N. Cleven of the University of Pittsburgh has found his field of specialization in the history of Latin America. J. A. O. Larsen of the University of Chicago is a student of representative government in classical times. Brynjolf J. Hovde of the University of Pittsburgh is interested chiefly in recent European history. John A. Gade, the well known New York architect, has written brilliantly on themes in history and art.

There are, of course, a number of other scholars of ability, promise, and achievement who might properly be mentioned along with those that have been named. In defense of these omissions one can only plead the limitations of space and the absence in some cases of certain information necessary to an intelligent choice. Still, even in its very imperfect form the list will prove abundantly that Norwegian scholarship in America is no longer either narrow or provincial.

The writer regrets exceedingly that he cannot give space to further detail about the work that these men and women are carrying forward — even if he were qualified to do so. The number of scholars is too large and their interests are too varied. There still remains a group, however, whose achievements cannot be passed without a more particular mention. It is not a large group — the list includes only thirteen names — but the scholars that are included are (or were) all eminent, each in his chosen field. It is a list that needs little explanation and probably no defense.

The Norwegian-Americans have to their credit one astronomer of high rank, John August Anderson of Pasadena, California. For a period of eight years Dr. Anderson taught astronomy at Johns Hopkins University. Since 1916 he has studied the stars at Mount Wilson Observatory, where he holds the position of physicist. It will be recalled that a dozen years ago Professor Michelson of Chicago published the results of a series of marvelous computations which opened new vistas in the field of astronomy; in the making of these computations Dr. Anderson had a large and important part. He is a leading authority on light.

Among our younger scholars one of the more prominent is Theodore C. Blegen, the energetic superintendent of the

Minnesota Historical Society. Dr. Blegen's field of interest is immigration and more particularly immigration from Norway. His labors in this field have already yielded a rich harvest, not only in briefer studies but also in longer works, all of which reveal the skilled hand of a master workman. His study in *Norwegian Migration to America,* of which the first volume appeared in 1931, promises to give the most complete and the most intelligible account of the subject that has thus far been published or planned.

In the field of philology there are today in the United States half a dozen men of unquestioned eminence: one of these is George Tobias Flom of the University of Illinois. No American scholar has searched deeper into the sources of Germanic speech than has Professor Flom. Of special value are his many studies in various forms of northern idioms, modern as well as medieval. From studies in primitive culture he has moved forward through the rural dialects of Norway to the early history of his people in the United States. Professor Flom is furthermore an accomplished paleographer, as is evidenced by his remarkable *Facsimile Edition of Konungs Skuggsjá* (1916).

One cannot prepare a list of this character without including the name of the late Knut Gjerset, who served for many years as professor of history at Luther College. The publication of Gjerset's *History of the Norwegian People* was a major event in the annals of historical scholarship in this country. The work filled a place that had long been vacant. It superseded all earlier accounts of Norwegian history in the English language and it is likely to remain long without a serious rival. What is said of the Norwegian history applies equally to his later *History of Iceland,* a volume which is in every respect a worthy companion to the earlier work. Professor Gjerset died in 1936.

In the field of medicine our most outstanding figure is Ludvig Hektoen, the famous pathologist of the University of Chicago. Dr. Hektoen is known so well and so widely in the Middle West that it is unnecessary to do more than to mention his name. He has achieved eminence not only in the treatment of disease, but as lecturer, author, and editor. His renown goes beyond the West: when the authorities of the National Research Council were casting about for a chairman to direct their medical section, they found their man in Dr. Hektoen.

Scholarship is not always a matter of books: sometimes it may find its finest expression in a great work of engineering. The writer therefore wishes to include in this group of eminent scholars a great engineer, the late Olaf Hoff, who died in 1924. He carried to successful completion such notable undertakings as the Detroit River tunnel and the subway under the Harlem River; but what gives him a real claim to a place among productive scholars is the fact that he devised the methods and the plans that made these undertakings possible. He was a citizen of New York.

In 1887 Aven Nelson, a young schoolman of Norwegian parentage, went out to the University of Wyoming to organize its work in botany. After nearly fifty years he is still actively in charge of this department. By dint of persistent research he has won recognition "as the foremost living authority on the classification of the Rocky Mountain plants." Dr. Nelson has also achieved distinction as a class-room teacher and administrative official. For ten years he was in charge of the executive office of the institution, first as acting president, then as president in his own right. He relinquished the presidency in 1922 but retained his professorship in botany.

In the profession of dentistry our outstanding representative for many years was the late Dr. Alfred Owre, sometime dean of the college of dentistry of the University of Minnesota. During the last few years of his life he held a corresponding position in Columbia University; but his great contribution to the science of dentistry was made in Minneapolis. In much of his work Dr. Owre was almost a pioneer. Mention should also be made of his labors for higher ethical standards in his profession, an undertaking which led to a conflict in which, unfortunately, he was not entirely victorious.

A writer who has displayed unusual productivity is Leonard Stejneger, who ranks as our foremost scholar in the natural sciences. Stejneger (at the age of eighty-five) is curator of biology at the United States National Museum, a branch of the Smithsonian Institution in the city of Washington. He has written extensively, in English and Norwegian, on animal life in many lands. Like Olaf Hoff he was born in Norway and received his formal education in European schools.

Eminent in chemistry and chemical engineering was Magnus Swenson, whose career closed in 1935. Dr. Swenson was a most remarkable man; as a scholar he was interested in the application of science to production. He is probably best known for the development of certain processes in manufacturing by which the production of sugar was materially increased. Swenson was also a man of large affairs in business and manufacturing. As a citizen he served his state in many capacities.

In the field of mathematics the most prominent student of Norwegian ancestry is Oswald Veblen of Princeton University. Dr. Veblen has added a number of significant works to the literature of his science and has received recognition for eminent scholarship not only from his fellow craftsmen in the United States but also from mathematicians in other lands.

Another member of the gifted Veblen family was Thorstein B. Veblen (an uncle of Oswald), who had a wide reputation for close thinking and brilliant writing. Dr. Veblen was an economist who was also very much at home in sociology. His first important work, *The Theory of the Leisure Class* (published in 1899), placed him at once in the front rank of American thinkers. He held teaching positions at the universities of Chicago and Missouri, Leland Stanford University, and the New School for Social Research (New York City). He died in 1929.

The list properly closes with the name of the late Fritz Wilhelm Woll, a highly cultured and thoroughly educated immigrant, who gave courses and carried on research in agricultural chemistry and animal nutrition, first at the University of Wisconsin and later in the agricultural college of the University of California. His research found publication in a long series of books, bulletins, reports, and articles, all of which evidence careful and profound scholarship. He died in 1922 at the age of fifty-seven.

These are the men to whom the writer wishes to pay a particular homage. They are the men who most directly have continued the traditions of the great work that was begun over the seas by Nils Henrik Abel, Sophus Bugge, Michael Sars, A. M. Schweigaard, and Peter Andreas Munch. They are the men to whom we owe such claim as we have to place and to rank in American scholarship. Most of them have, it is true, found their life work outside the Norwegian sphere of influence; but that was inevitable, and it was an outcome that none should need to regret.

This last observation leads directly to a highly pertinent question: Is there nothing that the organized forces of learning among the Norwegians of the Northwest can do to promote the type of scholarship that involves scientific research? It seems clear that an attempt to establish a graduate school would be futile, inasmuch as the Norwegian taxpayers are helping to maintain such institutions at the state universities. And yet, it is a task that seems well worth undertaking, one which the state institutions cannot very well maintain.

Much has been said in recent years about preserving the heritage of the Norwegian element. One way, and perhaps the only effective way, to preserve a racial heritage is to preserve its memorials. It is gratifying to find that significant steps have been taken in this direction in several important institutions. Real progress has been made and one has good reason to believe that even greater results will be achieved in the years before us.

One of the most interesting exhibits that the writer has seen in recent years is the work that is being done by interested individuals in Decorah, Iowa. Under the direction of Karl T. Jacobsen, the librarian at Luther College, the foundations have been laid for an important collection of books, newspapers, and official records in the library of that institution. A parallel activity was that of Professor Gjerset, who gathered into the Norwegian-American Museum a remarkable exhibit of tools and implements, household furniture, and home decorations; in short, whatever may serve to illustrate the Norwegian type of pioneer life. It is a collection that may acquire great significance.

Other important bodies of historical materials (and they are not narrowly historical) that the writer has been privileged to examine are those in the libraries of the great historical societies of Minnesota and Wisconsin and of the Norwegian-American Historical Association, the archives of which are housed at St. Olaf College. Less extensive, though of real value, is the collection in the library of Luther Theological Seminary in St. Paul. Lesser collections can be found in various parts of the country and as far east as Harvard University. It is likely that all our great libraries have in their possession notable bodies of Norwegian-American source materials, some of which can be rated as of great value.

The work should be carried further. The writer once believed that it might be possible to establish somewhere in the Northwest a library with stacks and shelves sufficiently ample to house all the Norwegian literature that is still in print or can be secured from antiquarian dealers. In addition it ought to contain copies of every book and pamphlet and newspaper published on this side of the ocean by men and women of Norwegian blood. It should have room and facilities for housing documentary materials of every sort consistent with the general purpose of the collection, for church records, for private correspondence, for personal memoirs, for anything that will help the student to understand the history of the Norwegian element in the American republic. Such an institution, if it could be established, would provide facilities for the study of Norse problems on both sides of the sea: not only the problems of history, but also those of the earlier culture, the linguistic developments, the national literature, the intellectual tendencies, the economic structure, and many more. And, what is not less important, the shelves of such a collection would demonstrate our achievement in every field of endeavor, in scholarship along with the rest.

A dozen years ago an institution of this character did not seem to lie beyond the bounds of possible attainment. Since then, however, much has occurred and many dreams have faded away. Perhaps it is wisest after all to depend on agencies that have already been established. But if these are to preserve our heritage and the evidence of our intellectual achievements, they will have to be rebuilt on a broader basis. Such an enlargement of current activities is, of course, possible only if these agencies are given a more cordial support than they have received in the past. To the writer the adequate promotion of the purpose outlined above would seem to be a duty to the land where we have found our home. It is the noblest contribution that we, as American citizens, can make to the cause of American scholarship.

THE CONVENTION RIOT AT BENSON GROVE, IOWA, IN 1876

In January, 1851, the legislature of Iowa was debating a proposal to create fifty new counties in the northern and western parts of the state, where, only five years before, the Potawatomi and various other Indian tribes had been in actual and undisputed possession. It is possible that here and there one might have discovered the home of a white man in this great area, but on the whole the fifty new counties were a vast tract of wild prairie, unoccupied and unsurveyed.

One of these new counties was Winnebago, a rectangular area lying approximately halfway between the eastern and western boundaries of the state and touching the Minnesota line on the north. In 1851 there was not a single white inhabitant in the Winnebago district, and none settled there before 1855, when Thomas Bearse built a log cabin in the wooded country about three-fourths of a mile east of the hills that were to be Forest City. Later in the same year several other homes were erected, nearly all in the broad woodland that covered the southeastern part of the county. More settlers went in during the years that followed. These early pioneers were nearly all native Americans: young, courageous, and enterprising men and women who had traveled in leisurely fashion across the land from homes that might be as far distant as Virginia or Vermont.

In 1856, the second year of settlement, a few Norwegian families found homes in the northeastern part of the county, in what was later to be organized as Norway Township.[1] This was the beginning of an important movement which

---

[1] Colburn [*Kolbein?*] Larson, Henrik Larson, Hans Knudson, and Lewis [*Lars?*] Nelson are said to have arrived in 1856. *History of Winnebago County and Hancock County, Iowa; a Record of Settlement, Organization, Progress, and Achievement,* 1:122 (Chicago, 1917).

was, in time, to extend into every part of the county. For ten years, however, Norwegian interest in the section remained of little consequence. In 1860 the census credited Winnebago County with 168 inhabitants; by 1865 the number had risen, but only to a meager 298. Nearly all those who were counted, moreover, were of native American stock. After the close of the Civil War, however, Norwegian settlers began to arrive in steadily growing numbers; the census of 1870 showed a population of 1,562. Americans were still going into the county, but the majority of those who went in during these five years bore Norwegian names.

In the late sixties a colony of Swedes was formed in the woods northeast of the site of Forest City. A few Germans had come into the county and the Irish were not entirely wanting. These elements were small and feeble, however, compared with the robust Norwegian settlements. At the close of the nineteenth century the population of Winnebago County must have been at least four-fifths Norwegian.

Among the earliest settlers was Robert Clark, who came to Winnebago in 1856. He had strength, ambition, and foresight, and he soon rose to first place in the little pioneer community. Perceiving that the high ground which lay on the edge of the woodland, west of Lime Creek, had possibilities as a town site, he secured the land and platted the village of Forest City. When the county was organized in 1857, the new town became the county seat, a distinction which to this day it has retained.

Forest City was and long continued to be the center of the native American strength and influence in the new community. For twenty years the settlement in and about the county seat controlled the public administration. " From the settlement of the county [in 1856] a majority of the settlers expected to make their living by holding township and county offices, or by hunting, trapping, or trading with the neighbors."[2] It was therefore generally believed, at least

---

[2] David Secor, " Reminiscence," in *History of Winnebago County and Hancock County*, 1:212.

among the foreign born, that the native element had organized to control offices and other political patronage in the county. That there was such an organization is quite likely, though it may have been entirely informal. Some of the leading citizens of Forest City were running for office at almost every election, and it is safe to assume that, as the body of naturalized citizens grew in numbers, the native Americans tried to close up their ranks and to tighten their grip on public affairs and offices.[3]

It was also generally believed among the new citizens that the county-seat "ring" was a venal concern, one that had developed a wonderful facility in the art of looting the public treasury. That the administration was often extravagant, according to the standards of pioneer life, is clear enough; but intentional dishonesty might be difficult to prove. "Money was scarce and they [*the pioneers*] used in its stead county, bridge, school house and road orders. Many county and township jobs were let at fabulous prices. The result was that these orders were sold as low as forty cents on the dollar."[4]

Although the courthouse group was dominated by men of American birth, its membership was not limited exclusively to citizens of the native stock. A few Norwegian families had traveled far and rapidly along the road to Americanization and had come to regard their interests as identical with those of their American neighbors. There were also a few young Norwegians who had fought for the flag on southern battlefields, and these men seem to have enjoyed the favor of both elements in the electorate; obviously a Civil War veteran could not be excluded from political life.

The first Norwegian to run for a county office was N. K. Landru, who was a candidate for recorder (register of deeds)

---

[3] In the eleven years from 1867 to 1877, one of these leaders was a candidate at eight elections, seeking the offices of auditor, treasurer, superintendent of schools, and clerk of the courts. He was successful five times.

[4] Secor, in *History of Winnebago County and Hancock County*, 1:212.

in the election of 1866. Landru was defeated by a small margin, but two years later he was successful and in 1870 he was given a second term. In 1867 his brother, H. K. Landru, a soldier with a good record, was elected sheriff. At the close of his term he was transferred to the newly established auditor's office, where he served for six years. Peter Lewis (Larson) succeeded to the sheriff's office in 1869; he proved a popular official and was re-elected three times. O. T. Severs was chosen county surveyor in 1873, but soon resigned the office; the following year he was elected clerk of the courts.

The first Norwegian to serve on the board of supervisors was Andrew N. Brones, who received the office in 1869.[5] Other early members of the county board were R. O. Haughland and W. O. Hanson, who were chosen in 1871 and 1872, respectively.

Of these men Lewis, Hanson, Severs, and the two Landrus were suspected by their fellow Norwegians of training with the "courthouse ring." They were also known to have become members, or adherents, of Reformed churches; and at a time when the American Norwegians, both learned and lay, were engaged in violent controversy over questions of Lutheran dogma, indifference to the old faith was bound to be resented. An even more disquieting circumstance was the popular belief that most of the "Norwegian Yankees" were members of the Masonic fraternity, the reports of whose mysterious doings filled many a simple-minded soul with horror and fear.

In the sixties and seventies the office of treasurer was regarded as the most desirable in the courthouse. David Secor held it for four years (1864–67). At the close of his second term it passed to Robert Clark, who held it until his death nearly nine years later. Clark was popular with

---

[5] In 1879 Brones was elected superintendent of schools and he served in this capacity for six years. The writer is indebted to him for important data used in the preparation of this paper. It may be added that Brones was one of three brothers who served in the Union army.

the Norwegians as well as with his own people. There was no contempt in his attitude toward foreigners; all voters were alike to him; and consequently he carried successive elections by decisive majorities.

Judge Clark's popularity was founded in large measure on a somewhat doubtful use of the public funds. The county had no bank where such funds could be deposited; but Clark carried on a form of real-estate and collection business which in some degree served the purpose of a banking institution. He lent money freely, especially when the applicant was in real need of assistance. It was widely believed that Clark's money-lending business was conducted with the county's money; but very few people saw any valid objection to this. If, on the day of settlement with the county board, the treasurer could produce the funds owing, it was considered nobody's business how the money had been used previously.

In making a loan Clark regarded native honesty as good security, and it may be that, if he had lived to the end of his term of office, the county would have suffered no great loss through his transactions. On August 12, 1876, however, he died suddenly. The news of his death produced a tremendous sensation. The intimate connection between his own private business and the treasurer's office now became a matter of the gravest concern. The county board was called into session and W. A. Burnap was appointed treasurer until a new official should be chosen.

As the voters looked forward to the November election they began to see clearly that the issue was not so much the financial condition of the county as the fate of the old organization. The indications were that the Norwegians were preparing to seize control at the courthouse. Their strength at the polls was growing at an almost alarming rate, for the courts were very liberal in admitting aliens to the rights of citizenship. Most of the applicants for naturalization had, indeed, to address the judge through an interpreter; but they were gradually becoming familiar with American ways and, what is more important, they were finding leaders of their own racial stock with whom they were able to discuss political affairs in their native language.

After much discussion, in which the candidates for the various offices appear to have participated prominently, it was agreed that the sentiment of the electorate should be tested in a mass convention. A central committee was formed, with C. D. Smith of Lake Mills as chairman. He promptly published a call for a convention to be held at Benson Grove, about six miles north of Forest City, on Saturday, October 21.

Doubtful though the outlook seemed to be, the native element probably was not without hope of being able to dominate this convention. The alien farmers had not yet become politically minded; they knew very little about American institutions and seemed quite indifferent to caucuses and other means for political maneuvering. There was, therefore, some reason to believe that the new voters would not appear in very large numbers at the proposed convention.

If such was the expectation of the native leaders, they were doomed to disappointment, for almost the entire voting strength of the county went to the meeting. In the issue of the *Winnebago Summit* for the week following the convention, the editor published the following discreet, though not very enlightening report:

The mass convention of Winnebago County last Saturday proved a failure. We will refrain from enumerating the causes of the defeat. They are well known to every citizen who was there. It will be sufficient to say that over 500 voters were in attendance. It was the largest gathering of the kind ever witnessed in our county. The leading candidates for Treasurer were Messrs. Larson, Peterson, and Smith; For Clerk of the Courts, Messrs Hanson, Isaacs, and Grassly; for Recorder, Law and Halversen; for Supervisor, Johnson, Bushnell, and Wadsworth.[6]

[6] *Winnebago Summit* (Forest City, Iowa), October 26, 1876. The Historical, Memorial, and Art Department of Iowa at Des Moines has a file of this paper.

It will be observed that the candidates for clerk of the courts were all Norwegians; but W. O. Hanson was regarded with favor by his neighbors in Forest City; he might even have been considered an organization candidate. It was believed, with some reason, that John Law would defeat M. C. Halvorsen, who had little strength among his own people. Knudt Johnson was expected to lead his two native American opponents in the race for the supervisor's office; as a veteran of the Civil War, Johnson had a following in both camps.

The real battle, however, was to be over the office of county treasurer. Two strong Norwegian candidates had come forward and neither showed any disposition to quit the field. It seemed quite likely, therefore, that C. D. Smith, who had many friends among the Norwegians in his part of the country, would secure the nomination.

Fearing that trouble might arise during the balloting, the promoters of the meeting had agreed that only the judges and other officials should be allowed to enter the polling place. The voters had to prepare their ballots in the schoolhouse yard and pass them through one of the windows to the officials in charge. Wishing to learn the outcome, most of the voters remained at Benson Grove until late in the afternoon. As the day advanced, it became evident that Smith would not win; but the name of the victor could not be foretold.

It is generally believed that a " gang " had been formed to break up the convention if it should appear that the Norwegians were getting the upper hand. At all events, there was a gang, composed chiefly of Irishmen and led by the three Bevins brothers, Jim, Frank, and Bill, doughty brawlers who had never been known to refuse a fight. Not far from the schoolhouse a covered wagon had driven up, from the interior of which the members of the gang and no doubt others, too, could obtain what was needed to prepare their spirits for the contest, if there was to be a contest.

The Norwegians had not organized to meet an attack; still, there were those among them who had no objection to joining their opponents in a mild or even a serious fracas. Throughout the day there had been much abusive palaver in which both sides indulged quite freely. Among those on the Norwegian side who talked most valiantly was one Hans Peterson, commonly known as *Kjæftehans*, who usually tried to live up to his reputation. At four o'clock Jim Bevins threw a decayed apple at Hans, which struck him in the eye. This was the signal for a general riot. Both sides flew to arms, which in this case meant fence rails and neck yokes. At the same time those who were not inclined to fight hurried to their wagons and started for the open road.

The casualties were many, but only a few were serious. Bloody faces were plentiful and one Irishman suffered a fractured skull. Among those who were driving away during the riot was the Reverend J. M. Dahl, a Lutheran pastor of considerable prominence at the time.[7] A terrified Norseman, who was fleeing from the menace of a fence rail carried in the strong hands of Jim Bevins, sought refuge in the pastor's buggy, which he was sure would be respected. But Jim, who had never stood in great awe of the clergy, struck at the two men and broke the rail over the clergyman's broad back. "Old Dahl just grunted 'Woof' and drove on."[8]

The members of the gang had fighting qualities of no mean order, but their opponents were too numerous and finally drove them from the field. The riot brought disaster to the old organization. Though it is quite unlikely that the leaders of the native element were in any way responsible

[7] J. M. Dahl was an interesting character. At one time he had served in the mission field and he came to be known as "Indi-Dahl." Though not a great preacher, he was very successful in organizing churches; at one time his parish extended into four counties. He was also noted for intelligent farming and for unusual physical strength.

[8] The writer is indebted to O. M. Peterson of Leland, Iowa, for information as to what happened at the convention. Mr. Peterson's father was one of the candidates for the treasurer's office.

for the riot, it was easy to credit the rumor that the gang had been hired by the courthouse crowd. A feeling of strong resentment swept over the county and when the Scandinavian farmers went to the polls on November 7, two weeks after the convention, they went with a determination to vote, as far as possible, for men of their own speech and race.

The native Americans at the county seat, realizing that public sentiment was at a high tension, made sure that there would be no riotous performances in Forest City on the day of election. The editor of the *Summit* reported a very satisfactory poll: " To the credit of Forest City the election on Tuesday passed off very peaceably and pleasantly. There was no liquor sold in town during the whole day. Sobriety and order reigned supreme."[9] William Larson, W. O. Hanson, John Law, and Knudt Johnson were the successful candidates. The vote for treasurer resulted as follows: William Larson, 206; C. D. Smith, 183; and Mikkel Peterson, 158.

William Larson was honest and capable, but he was also something of a " grouch," and his year in the treasurer's office did not add to his political strength. In the election of the following year he was defeated by Mikkel Peterson, his rival of the year before. At the same time Norwegian candidates secured the offices of sheriff and of supervisor; but the auditor and the superintendent of schools, both of whom were native Americans, were re-elected to their respective offices. This, however, was entirely in accord with the traditions of Winnebago County politics, which normally allowed a competent official the satisfaction of a second term.

By the two elections of 1876 and 1877 the leaders of the immigrant element had come into almost complete control of the county administration, and the same element has kept this control to the present. For a number of years it

9 *Winnebago Summit*, November 9, 1876.

was exceedingly difficult for a native American citizen to secure an important county office. The Norwegians showed little interest in the functions of the offices of surveyor and coroner, and they were willing to leave these positions to native Americans. Frequently, too, the sheriff and the superintendent of schools were chosen from the native citizenship: in the forty years following the election of 1876 three native Americans and three Norwegians served in the capacity of sheriff. The more important administrative offices of auditor, treasurer, recorder, and clerk of the courts, however, were usually given to Norwegians. In the same period of forty years thirty-one men, of whom only four were native Americans, were elected to these positions. The history of the county board tells a similar tale: of twenty-four men elected to the office of supervisor in the years from 1876 to 1916, twenty-one were Norwegians.

Though this record might lead one to draw the conclusion that the political development of Winnebago County has been directed by what may be called " clan sentiment," such is scarcely the case. That, in the seventies, there was such a feeling in both camps cannot be denied; on that point the writer's own memory is clear and distinct. But, like most emotions, this feeling could not long be kept at white heat; racial antagonism could not long endure the wearing force of daily contact, and soon it disappeared altogether.

Nevertheless, a Norwegian name long was, and perhaps still is, an asset in the political business of the county. It is a long time since a non-Norwegian was at any disadvantage in competition for office because of his racial origin; still, in a locality where four-fifths of the population belongs to a definite racial group, one may naturally expect to find that leadership in public affairs has come to remain with that particular group.

The history of the literary achievements of the Norwegian
element in the New World begins with the publication of Ole
Rynning's famous "America Book," which came from the
press in 1838.[1] A year later a printer in Drammen brought
out a "Description of a Journey to North America," and
into the West, by Ole Nattestad, another young immigrant
who had been Rynning's fellow traveler on the journey from
Detroit to Illinois.[2] It is possible that Nattestad's book was
written, at least in part, before Rynning began to prepare
his "True Account," but the latter has the priority of publication and proved the more important work.

These two pamphlets (for they were scarcely more than
that) were in the nature of "guides" to prospective immigrants and were read widely, especially in southern Norway. But though useful and effective, they can be classed as
literature only when that term is used in its more inclusive
sense. The same must be said of the books, pamphlets, and
journalistic writings of Norwegian-American origin which
found their way to the press during the forty years following. The harvest was considerable but the grain was not of
the finer sort. The greater part of this material was of a
religious character; at least it was produced in the interest
of religion. Some of the authors aimed at spiritual edifica-
tion, but the greater number wrote from the impulse of
controversy, of which there was much among the Norwegian
pioneers in those early days.

---

[1] *Sandfærdig beretning om Amerika* (Christiania, 1838). The preface is
dated Illinois, February 13, 1838, and is signed by the author. Rynning's book
has been republished with a translation by the Norwegian-American Historical
Association. (Theodore C. Blegen, ed., *Ole Rynning's True Account of America*,
Minneapolis, 1926.)

[2] Ole K. Nattestad, *Beskrivelse over en reise til Nordamerika begyndt den 8de
April, 1837,* etc. (Drammen, Norway, 1839).

It may seem strange and almost incredible that Norwegians should have been settled in considerable numbers on American soil for nearly fifty years before anyone among them undertook to write anything in the form of literary fiction. The cause of this is not far to seek: the energies of the pioneer were engaged first with the conquest of the soil and next with the building of a new social order. The materials for such building were to a large extent brought from over the sea; but they had to be fitted into the forms demanded by the new environment, and that proved at times to be a difficult and often a very delicate task.

The first Norwegian to find a place in American literature was Hjalmar Hjorth Boyesen, who went to the West in 1869. Boyesen was of the Norwegian intelligentsia and had received his education in the best schools of his native land. Youthful and buoyant, he was ready for almost any sort of adventure in the field of intellectual endeavor and he had been assured that in the great Republic opportunity would not be lacking.

It would be natural to conclude that a man with Boyesen's training and background would soon find a place for himself in the front rank of the growing and highly respectable and aggressive company of Norwegian university graduates and other intellectuals who were assiduously cultivating the ideals of Norsedom in the rich soil of the West. The young man's future, however, did not lie in this field. While engaged in editorial work in Chicago he used his native idiom as the only practical form of expression; but his journalistic activities were a matter of scarcely more than a year;[3] at the end of that period he entered upon a professorial career in which he continued with only brief interruptions till his death twenty-five years later.

Meanwhile, during his stay in Chicago, Boyesen was perfecting his knowledge of English; he achieved a complete mastery of it in an amazingly short time. It was his fate

[3] See *post*, p. 88-92.

to become more widely known and more generally appreciated as an author than as an educator. He wrote all his books in the English language. This does not mean that he surrendered his interest in things Norwegian; the fact that he was able to maintain this interest and to weave Norwegian materials into his books enabled him to become a well-known author—one of the most popular American authors of his own day.

Boyesen's literary career is reviewed elsewhere in this volume and it is therefore not necessary to discuss his writings at this point.[4] Mention should be made, however, of his first novel, *Gunnar*, inasmuch as it lies at the very threshold of our subject. *Gunnar* is a decidedly youthful effort; still, one is surprised to find a story of such unique quality written by an immigrant after a stay of scarcely more than a year in the New World. It ran as a serial in the *Atlantic Monthly* in 1873 and appeared in book form the following year.

While it remains true that *Gunnar* was the first novel written by a Norwegian immigrant, it can scarcely be classified as belonging to the genre that one may call Norwegian-American literature. Boyesen spent most of his American years east of the Allegheny Mountains; he was consequently not in close touch with his fellow Norsemen in the spreading settlements of the Northwest and had little knowledge of the forces and movements that were shaping their lives.[6] His literary purpose was to give the American public some acquaintance with Norwegian life and some insight into the Norse character. It is to his great credit that this purpose was in a large measure achieved.

Very much the same can be said of another young man who published a notable book in the year that saw the first

[4] See *post*, p. 96-118.
[5] The story was first published by Osgood and Company, Boston. Later editions came from the press of Charles Scribner's Sons.
[6] On Boyesen's novel *Falconberg*, the scene of which is laid in Minnesota, see *post*, p. 103–106.

edition of Boyesen's novel. Rasmus Bjørn Anderson was a little more than a year older than his Norwegian contemporary. Like Boyesen he had had the advantage of university training, though scarcely a training equal to that provided by the universities of Europe. Anderson, too, wished to make his fellow citizens aware of the wonders of Norway, particularly of those that belonged to the romantic past. His first book, *America Not Discovered by Columbus*, dealt with the difficult problem of the Vinland voyages.[7] His later works were also concerned with subjects from across the sea. Except in the journalistic arena (and to a lesser degree in the field of local history) Anderson has not dealt with the problems of his brethren in rural America.

The significance of these two young writers, Boyesen, the cultured professor in the East,[8] and Anderson, the militant professor in the West,[9] seems to lie for present purposes not so much in what they achieved in their own fields as in the impulse they gave to literary and other intellectual work in related fields. With their writings a new chapter begins in the history of art and thought in the Norwegian colonies and the year 1874 therefore becomes a date of real significance.

A third writer who belongs to the same group is Bernt Askevold, an immigrant from Søndfjord, a romantic district in western Norway just north of Sogn. Born in 1846, Askevold was two years older than Boyesen and a few months younger than Anderson. He came to America in 1873 and located in Decorah, Iowa. He was there in 1874 when the two volumes mentioned above came from the

---

[7] Chicago, 1874.

[8] In 1873 Boyesen secured an assistant professorship in north European languages (which seem to have included German) at Cornell University, and he held this position for six years. In 1881 he was appointed to an instructorship in German at Columbia College; he was holding a professorship in that subject at the time of his death (1895).

[9] Anderson was instructor in languages and later professor of Scandinavian languages in the University of Wisconsin, 1869-83.

press. Doubtless he shared the enthusiasm of those among his countrymen who had literary interests and who rejoiced in these new voices which had begun to tell of the marvels of the North.

In that same year Askevold assisted at the launching of a new venture that was to have much meaning for the Norwegian pioneer. Brynild Anundsen had just perfected his plans to publish a weekly newspaper which was to be called *Decorah posten*. Askevold was Anundsen's first editor and for this position he was fairly well qualified. He had received a measure of training in the higher schools of his native land, and had served for a year as teacher in the public schools of Bergen. He spent a year as student in Luther College and later studied theology at Luther Seminary in Madison, Wisconsin. He was ordained to the Lutheran ministry in 1882. But most of this lay in the future.[10] In 1874 he was merely a young "newcomer" with a strong desire to learn and an equally strong desire to express himself in written speech.

It is important to note that in his training and in his later professional duties Askevold kept close to his own people; as student, as journalist, and as Lutheran pastor he continued to use, one might say he was compelled to use, his native idiom. One cannot doubt that to a man of Askevold's ambitions the wide publicity given to the work of his two greater contemporaries proved a powerful stimulus. At any rate, he was soon at work on a novel, in which he sought to reproduce certain aspects of life in his native homeland. He called his book *Hun Ragnhild, eller billeder fra Søndfjord* (Ragnhild, or Pictures from Søndfjord).[11] Askevold's book was the first novel in the United States to be written and published in the Norwegian language. As such it is an important landmark in our history, more im-

[10] Askevold developed a notable activity in literary lines, both fictional and didactic. For a list of his writings see *Who's Who among Pastors* (Minneapolis, 1928). He died in 1926 at the age of eighty.

[11] Chicago, 1876.

portant than *Gunnar,* inasmuch as the author directed his appeal not to the cultivated American public in the East but to the untutored men and women in the log houses on the northwestern prairies.

II

A few months after Askevold's arrival in Decorah another young man came to the same town to take an inconspicuous position as prescription clerk in a drug store. This was Tellef Grundysen, a young Setesdøl from a farm in Fillmore County, Minnesota. Grundysen did not come with college or university training; his formal education was indeed very slight. What instruction he had received in the Norwegian language was such as would be given in a pioneer home, supplemented by preparation for the rite of confirmation. There is no evidence that the young drug clerk was ever taught any of the rules that govern the writing of his native speech; still, he achieved what no one before him had achieved: he wrote *Fra begge sider af havet* (From Both Sides of the Sea), the first novel to deal with life in a Norwegian settlement on this side of the ocean. He was, therefore, the first in a notable series that contains such names as H. A. Foss, Kristofer Janson, Peer Strømme, Simon Johnson, Waldemar Ager, and O. E. Rølvaag.

Tellef Grundysen first saw the light in 1854 in Bygland parish, Setesdal. His father, Grunde Tellefsen, was born on Langei farm in Austad parish, and his mother, Gro Arnesdatter, was from Valle parish higher up the valley. They were both of the cotter (or "houseman") class and their history was no doubt the ancient and much too common story of dire poverty and great hardship. A cotter was allowed a cabin (hence the term houseman) and a little strip of soil — enough, perhaps, for a fair patch of potatoes. The farmer from whom he held his "place" had a right, when need was, to command all his labor, in return, of course, for wages; but these were always small and wholly inadequate to supply the needs of a poor man's family.

Grunde Tellefsen found a little farm to work, but after trying for several years to maintain himself on another man's land, he determined to emigrate. The long journey was undertaken in 1861. Traveling down the valley to Christiansand, the family took passage on a sailing vessel, which after a time brought its passengers safe to land in Quebec. Thence the journey went on westward to Fillmore County in southern Minnesota, where the long experience ended, sixteen dreary weeks after the departure from Setesdal and Christiansand.

Norwegians had begun to enter Fillmore County ten years earlier, and strong settlements were in the process of formation.[12] The Tellefsen group was therefore among men and women of its own nationality, possibly among friends and acquaintances, for there were many immigrants from Setesdal in southern Minnesota.[13] Tellefsen built his home once more on rented land; but after a few years he acquired a farm of his own, and he and his family were soon firmly rooted in the new soil.

The farm was located in York Township not far from the Iowa line. Here young Tellef, who was now about ten years old, was to spend another decade until he was ready to make his own way in the world. Here he received most of his training, at least in Norwegian, which he had no doubt learned to read while his parents were still living in the old valley. There were books in the Tellefsen home, and more were added as the years went by. They were largely of a devotional character; but in the little collection there were also historical writings and some books of poetry and fiction.

Tellef's religious instruction was no doubt based on the

[12] See Martin Ulvestad, *Nordmændene i Amerika*, 79-82 (Minneapolis, 1907).
[13] Some time in the later sixties a Norwegian Lutheran congregation was organized in the York settlement and was called Sætersdal, a name which it still retains.

conventional study of Pontoppidan's *Forklaring* (Explanation) and some elementary work on sacred and church history. At the age of fifteen he was confirmed by Tobias Larsen of the Norwegian Synod, who served a group of congregations in that part of the county. All the leading branches of Norwegian Lutheranism were represented in Fillmore County; but the Tellefsen family evidently favored the more conservative standards and adhered to the church that most resembled the establishment in their native land.

For about four months of the year Tellef attended the public school in the neighborhood, where he learned the English language and studied such subjects as were usually taught in the common school seventy years ago. There could, of course, be no attendance during the summer. In those days there was little machinery on a pioneer farm: the seeding, the mowing, the reaping, the binding, and much of the other work had to be done by hand with the aid of the scythe, the cradle, and similar implements. It is true that such labor had its compensations: it kept the workman close to nature and rural nature is not only wonderful but to some souls it is also very enlightening and even stimulating. And yet, much of the work on a pioneer farm was of a deadening character and had little value for one who might be looking forward to intellectual pursuits.

At the age of nineteen (probably in 1873) Grundysen left his home in Minnesota to attend a business college in Madison, Wisconsin. On completing his course he went to Decorah to take a clerkship, as stated earlier. He remained with his bottles and his medicines for about two years. One cannot help wondering whether he came under the influence of Bernt Askevold, whom he certainly must have known by sight and by reputation, if not more intimately; but on this point the writer has no information.

However this may be, Grundysen, on his return to his Fillmore County home, set about writing a novel. This was in 1876, the year when Askevold's *Ragnhild* came from the press. For one who had no technical preparation for such work, this undertaking must have been a discouraging experience; but young Grundysen persisted and after a time the story was completed. He sent the manuscript to the publishers of *Skandinaven,* who dealt in books and also published an occasional volume on their own account. To the author's great delight, perhaps also to his great surprise, the manuscript was accepted for publication.

Fra begge sider af havet appeared in the book trade in 1877.[14] It was a simple straightforward story of the experiences of a Norwegian family in Setesdal and in southern Minnesota. It made no pretense to literary art and a modern critic would find little in the novel to commend. But it was exactly the sort of tale that a pioneer public was prepared to enjoy. To prove its popularity one need only state that a second edition was brought out in 1882 and a third in 1896.[15]

Tellef Grundysen's later career has little interest for the student of literature. In the later seventies " Jim " Hill had begun to advertise the attractions of the Red River Valley and Norsemen were responding in large numbers to the invitation to settle on what was said to be the richest soil in the West. Among those who went to the valley in the earlier years of the migration was Tellef Grundysen. Soon after his book was published he made preparations to leave his Fillmore County home and he moved to Grand Forks County, Dakota Territory, where he secured a farm under the Homestead Act.

Until his farming could become productive he engaged in various occupations; for a time he served as a public-school teacher. His neighbors recognized him as a young man of parts and in 1879, when he was still only twenty-five years of age, they elected him county commissioner, an

[14] The only available copy of the first edition, so far as the writer has been able to learn, is in the Haldor Hanson collection in the Luther College library.
[15] There is a copy of the second edition in the Luther College library and one of the third in the library of the Minnesota Historical Society.

office he held for two years. In addition to the satisfaction of being elected to an important office, he had the gratification of finding himself chosen by a large majority vote.

Two years later, in 1881, the young author entered the journalistic field with a new Norwegian weekly which he called *Grand Forks tidende*. Being wholly unacquainted with the details of the newspaper business, he was unable to make this venture a success; and after two years of trying experiences he was glad to dispose of the paper. The purchaser, T. Gulbrandsen, continued the publication of *Tidende* for several years; but in 1888 he moved the paper to Minneapolis and merged it with *Minneapolis tidende*, which he had begun to publish the year before.

The young Norseman did not remain long in the Red River country. In 1883 the completion of the Northern Pacific Railway was celebrated with pomp and ceremony. The Far West was calling and Tellef Grundysen obeyed the call. He had recently taken a wife and the two now set out for the coast. There he found employment in some form of engineering and continued in that service till his retirement a few years ago. So far as the writer knows he is still living, though his address has not been learned.[16]

III

In the decade of the seventies the outstanding figure in Norwegian literature was Bjørnstjerne Bjørnson. Bjørnson had begun his career as a novelist in 1857 with *Synnøve Solbakken*, a story of rural life in Norway. This was followed in due course by *Arne* in 1858 and *En glad gut* (A

[16] Most of the information about Tellef Grundysen and his career has been contributed by Arny Grundysen of Fisher, Minnesota. The writer is indebted also to Professor Richard Beck of the University of North Dakota; F. W. Arneson of the publication department of *Skandinaven*, Chicago; Carl G. O. Hansen of *Minneapolis tidende*, Minneapolis; Martin Ulvestad of Seattle, Washington; Karl T. Jacobsen, librarian at Luther College, Decorah, Iowa; and Dr. Theodore C. Blegen, superintendent of the Minnesota Historical Society, St. Paul, all of whom have contributed information or given other forms of assistance.

TELLEF GRUNDYSEN

Happy Boy) in 1860. Bjørnson also published a series of shorter stories that were all of the same general class as his longer novels. It cannot be denied that Bjørnson's pictures of rural life are highly idealized; but after the critic has pointed out this defect and possibly other faults, he is usually willing to grant that these so-called " peasant stories " are real gems of literary art and richly deserve the popularity that they have achieved.

More important for present purposes is the fact that the great author developed something of a formula for the writing of such tales. This proved a godsend to his less gifted imitators, of whom he had many. The formula appears in its perfection in the story of Øyvind, the " happy boy." Øyvind is a cotter's son, a strong, healthy, intelligent, and capable young man; but his family is poor and his prospects are anything but bright. He is in love with the granddaughter of a prominent farmer, who cannot for a moment consider a cotter lad as a possible grandson-in-law. The schoolmaster, a kindly old man, befriends the bright lad, and through his efforts the boy becomes a student at a school of agriculture. In this way Øyvind wins prestige in the parish and is able to break down the caste feeling that has kept him from his beloved. In the end all is well.

One cannot read Boyesen's *Gunnar* without being reminded of Bjørnson's art in almost every chapter. His prologue on the mountain is reminiscent of the opening chapter in Bjørnson's *Arne*, though there has been no actual borrowing of details. Gunnar, a cotter lad, loves Ragnhild, the beautiful daughter of a proud and wealthy mother. But Gunnar is not merely a capable boy, he is an artist. He finds his way to the capital, where he proves his genius and wins a gold medal. Ragnhild's mother is forced to yield and the story ends with a glimpse of Gunnar and his bride on a journey to the art centers of the continent.

A novel dealing with rural life in Norway apparently must have a poet among its characters. Some of Bjørnson's

heroes and heroines have striking abilities in poetic composition. Boyesen has provided one in Rhyme-Ola, whose
poems are not entirely to be discarded, though they are not
so fine as those of Øyvind or Arne.

Bernt Askevold's imitation of his great contemporary was
even more apparent. Lars Røisæt has a very lovely daughter
Ragnhild, whom he wishes to give to a rich husband. But
the inevitable cotter lad is near at hand and Ragnhild loves
him dearly. The author therefore adopts Bjørnson's expedient and sends Ola Øren to a normal school. His return
to the parish as a seminarist is almost an event and the
caste feeling begins to yield. The situation is further sim-
plified by the death of Ragnhild's only brother, by which
event she becomes heiress to the farm. Ola is finally accepted as a son-in-law and very soon rises to leadership in
all the larger affairs of the parish.

Askevold's novel moves on a much lower plane than
does Boyesen's *Gunnar*. The story develops naturally, but
the dialogue is often labored and stiff and the characters
have no real distinction. The poems that are scattered
about among the chapters have little energy. Now and
then, however, the narrative rises to greater heights. The
author's description of a storm that swept the fjord and
wrought destruction on sea and shore shows real power.
The story is wholesome and not without real interest. No
doubt it had a strong appeal for those who looked back to
ancestral homes in the region of the many fjords.

Tellef Grundysen's novel differs from *Gunnar* and *Ragnhild* in at least one essential respect: the scene is laid
partly in Norway and partly in Minnesota; it therefore actually is " from both sides of the sea." Boyesen and Askevold close their stories with marriages: in Grundysen's
novel the marriage of the heroine comes before the story is
half told. The main lines of the narrative are projected into
a new environment and come to a focus in the solution of a
crime.

In the portion of the book that deals with Norway, Grundysen has Bjørnson as a guide but he is not a consistent follower. It is true that the clash of the emotions of the cotter and the aspirations of the wealthy farmer takes place in the story and that the cotter finally wins; but this part of the narrative concerns not the heroine but her friend Sigrid, who belongs to the wealthier class. Anne Granemo, the woman about whose life the story is built, comes from a cotter's home and marries a man of her own station in life.

Anne is an attractive young woman who is perhaps in her early twenties. She lives with her mother on a little " place " attached to an important farm in Setesdal. When the story opens, she is about to enter service on a large farm in a neighboring parish. The episodes in the first part of the novel are concerned chiefly with her experiences in this employment and with friendships that she forms in her employer's household. The marriage of the farmer's daughter Sigrid is one of the most interesting parts of the story; a Setesdal wedding is known throughout Norway as a picturesque event and the author makes fair use of his opportunity.

Anne also makes friendships in less prominent homes and one of these results in her marriage to Gunnar, a young man of promise but of little wealth. She and her husband find a farm which the author calls Søgaarden (The South Farm), where they remain for some years. In the meantime two of Anne's brothers have emigrated and the letters that come from the New World tell of many cattle and lovely farms. The " America fever " is soon kindled in the humble Setesdal home and before long Anne and her family are on their way to take passage on an emigrant ship that lies waiting in Christiansand.

After an account of pioneer life in Fillmore County, the story becomes concerned with a forgery which cost the Søgaarden family the snug sum of twenty thousand dollars.

This part of the novel was probably suggested by one of the many melodramatic tales that were current in the decade following the Civil War. One of Anne's brothers (who does not otherwise figure in the narrative) finds his death on a battlefield in Virginia. He leaves most of his estate — in Beloit, Wisconsin — to his sister. His brother Ole, a weak, unprincipled man, who allows himself to be dominated by an evil-minded wife, determines to get the money for himself. With the aid of a corrupt official and the holder of a mortgage against his brother's property, he succeeds in raising the sum involved in the debt from five hundred to twenty thousand dollars. In the final settlement of the estate, Anne receives almost nothing.

Ten years go by and Theodore, the oldest son in the family, has entered the years of young manhood. His parents send him to Madison where he takes up the study of medicine. Some years later in his professional capacity he is called to the bedside of a "Mr. Johnson" who is dying and wishes to relieve his conscience while there is still time. Johnson proves to be the one who held the mortgage that Ole Granemo abstracted and replaced with a forged instrument. The dying scoundrel makes a full confession. The young doctor passes the information on to the authorities and his uncle is speedily tried and sent to prison.

The deathbed scene (in which the narrative reaches its climax) is not entirely convincing. Johnson is remarkably clear and precise both in speech and memory for one who has already felt the hand of death. A touch of drama appears at the last when it is discovered that Johnson is the assumed name of a highly undesirable wooer who had proved a great annoyance to Sigrid, Anne's friend of thirty years before in old Setesdal.

One would not be justified in making any great claims for Grundysen's novel as a work of literary art. The characters are drawn with little skill; most of the episodes are quite commonplace both in development and in outcome;

and the author's attempts to describe the marvels of nature, whether in action or in repose, are usually wanting in the essential qualities of beauty and strength. It is true, of course, that he is wholly concerned with ordinary men and women engaged in the ordinary affairs of life. His characters are all simple folk and he tries to deal with them on their own level. Most of those whom we meet on the American scene are defective in the essentials of good character. The heroine is indeed an upright woman of good parts, and the author does not attempt to make her anything else.

The atmosphere of his tale is, therefore, one of stark reality. Unlike his contemporaries in the Norwegian field, who all had a strong tendency to idealize, Grundysen strove after a truthful realism in all his episodes. At the same time no critic would care to affirm that the author was wanting in imaginative power; there are pages here and there in his novel that show the contrary to be true. Grundysen's account of the landslide, of the Setesdal wedding, of the toilsome journey to the seaport, and of the raging storm on the ocean, all have undeniable merit, though they seem to show that the artist worked in too great a haste to produce a finished picture.

In a certain sense *Fra begge sider af havet* is a family saga, the family concerned being the author's own. A great deal of the material used in constructing the story appears to have been gathered from Grundysen's own stock of memories and from that of his parents. The experiences of emigration, the long and stormy voyage over the sea, the early impressions of Minnesota, the renting of land, and the building of a new home on freehold soil — all these facts appear to have close parallels in the history of the Grundysen household. Theodore Sœgarden [17] and Tellef Grundysen both go to Madison to study. One becomes a physician and writes prescriptions; the other finds employment in a drug store where he fills prescriptions and dispenses

[17] Theodore Søgaarden spelled his name in this way.

patent medicines. One must not, of course, force the argument; all writers draw on their memories and in that way often succeed in imparting realism to what is essentially fiction. The difference in Grundysen's case appears to be merely that he has drawn more heavily on a fund of actual experience than authors usually do. That this conclusion is valid seems evident from the reception that the novel had in the author's own community. His neighbors had little difficulty in identifying the principal characters in the story, and they found much in the book that they knew was based on actual facts and occurrences.[18] But the story of the crime — the forgery, the jury trial, and the penalty — that was a different matter. Such deeds had never been committed in their settlement. That part of the novel was malicious invention; it could be nothing else.

Unfortunately Grundysen had stated in his preface that his narrative was a true story. This statement his readers in the Fillmore neighborhood took seriously, and they feared that others would regard it in the same light. If they did, what would then become of the Setesdøls' reputation for honesty, integrity, and upright dealings with their fellow men?

A year after the publication of the book twelve men, all from the Setesdøl settlement in southern Minnesota, joined in a statement condemning the novel as a base fabrication and a libel on the immigrants from the author's own valley. They were willing to admit that their countrymen had certain deplorable habits; but they were not criminals. No man of Setesdøl blood had ever committed a penitentiary offense. Consequently they were sure that no man of their racial stock could be found in any state prison anywhere in the land. Moreover, no Setesdøl among those who fell in the Civil War had ever possessed so much as twenty thousand dollars. So the story was not only a fabrication in large part, it was also utterly improbable.[19]

[18] Letter of K. J. Nomland in *Skandinaven*, April 12, 1879.
[19] The protest was published in *Skandinaven* for December 31, 1878.

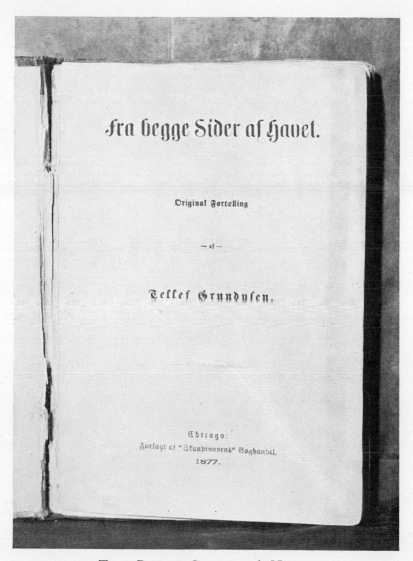

TITLE PAGE OF GRUNDYSEN'S NOVEL
[From a copy in the library of Luther College, Decorah, Iowa]

It is possible that the hostility of his old neighbors may have had something to do with Grundysen's decision to migrate to the newer lands in the Red River country; at any rate when the Fillmore protest was published he was already a resident of a large and growing Setesdøl colony spanning the famous river in its middle course. In the new environment there was no feeling that Tellef Grundysen had been unkind to his race or to his kindred. In the discussion that followed the appearance of the protest his new neighbors rallied to his defense.[20] Grundysen, they argued, had simply exercised the right of a novelist to draw on the resources of his imagination. The fact that his villain was from Setesdal had no significance. It surely could not be interpreted as a slur on the character of the author's people.

It has been stated above that Grundysen's book, when studied from the viewpoint of the literary critic, is not remarkable in any respect. But when the novel is read in the light of its own history and when all the circumstances of its origin are taken into account, even the severest critic is likely to allow that the work is, after all, a notable performance. Attention has already been called to the fact that Grundysen was lacking in all the ordinary qualifications required for successful literary work. No doubt the manuscript had to be carefully edited in the publisher's office; but the editorial reader evidently concluded that the story would interest the public for which it was written, and the conclusion proved to be sound.

Except in so far as later writers have adopted his general plan, Grundysen appears to have had no conscious imitators. The novel *Husmandsgutten* [21] (The Cotter Lad) is built on somewhat the same lines as Grundysen's story; but in the development of the narrative there is, after all, very little

---

[20] The discussion had begun some months before the twelve had made their protest public. *Skandinaven*, September 10, October 1, and November 19, 1878; April 28 and July 29, 1879.

[21] H. A. Foss, *Husmandsgutten, en fortælling fra Sigdal* (Decorah, Iowa, 1885). Hans Anderson Foss emigrated in 1877 and went to the Red River Valley the same year.

resemblance. Foss had greater possibilities as an author than Grundysen. He had a more vigorous imagination and wrote a more energetic style. Unfortunately he had a tendency to make literature serve the purpose of propaganda; and as a propagandist he would sometimes include materials that were scarcely in good taste.[22]

To the student of literary history *Husmandsgutten* has much less of real interest than Grundysen's narrative "From Both Sides of the Sea." In the distinctly Norwegian part of his story Foss employs the Bjørnson formula in all its essential details. The cotter lad does not indeed become a student, but all the necessary arrangements have been made when the plan is wrecked by the malicious opposition of the young man's future father-in-law. So young Haugen decides to emigrate. But his career in the New World is not that of a typical Norwegian pioneer, and as a contribution to the literature of Norwegian-American life Foss's narrative is not very important.

The Søgaarden family, on the other hand, is quite conventional in its experiences in a pioneer settlement. Moreover, it is the first family of Norse origin whose experiences have been recorded in this way. Tellef Grundysen saw what Boyesen, Askevold, and even Foss did not appreciate, namely, that a Norwegian-American literature should have as its chief concern the life and the activities of the Norwegian group in its new environment. He has had many followers, most of them greater and more highly gifted than he. But he was the first to break the soil. In his field Tellef Grundysen was the pioneer.

[22] As for example when he quotes an inscription on a tombstone which records the fact that the deceased had died from indulging too freely in strong drink.

Forty years ago Professor Frederick Jackson Turner advanced a theory of American development which has revolutionized the study and the writing of our national history. The terms of the Turner hypothesis are too well known to require a restatement. One need only call to mind that his views were concerned with the progress of settlement from coast to coast and were applicable to the history of New England as well as to the newer story of Illinois and the Northwest.

Turner's outlook was national; but, as his studies progressed, he seemed to discover a peculiar significance in the movement from the Appalachian highlands into and across the Mississippi Valley, a movement which showed great energy about 1790. In the century following, men and women of colonial stock, largely though not exclusively of British ancestry, built a mighty empire in the Mississippi basin, an achievement so remarkable that one searches in vain for an adequate parallel.

The achievement was not theirs alone. The native pioneers brought resourceful leadership, intelligent energy and workable plans; but without efficient help from other sources they could never have built as they did. The entire white population in 1790 was something more than three million. To what extent these would have multiplied, without additions by immigration, cannot be determined. Estimates vary; but whatever figure is accepted, it seems clear that the native white American stock, the stock that traces its ancestry back to Revolutionary times, is now a decreasing minority.

Help came from over the sea. The peoples of Europe bestirred themselves and soon there was much activity in

European ports. Irish, Germans, and Scandinavians came first, along with important contingents from Great Britain. Other nations came later. Though scarcely more than a trickle at first, the movement grew in volume until, about the turn of the century, it had swelled to a mighty torrent fed from a hundred sources and flowing forth from almost every part of the civilized world.

Such statistics as are available seem to indicate that at least thirty-six million aliens have landed in our ports since 1790. Most of these were men and women still in the years of youth. Most of them established families and had descendants; some of them had many descendants. In its earlier stages this human flood found a convenient outlet in the upper states of the West, where land was cheap or even free. As this area filled up, the newcomers turned their faces toward the cities. This was, of course, nothing new: from the very beginning a considerable number of immigrants had been attracted to the urban centers.

Professor Turner saw distinctly that the immigration movement was a highly significant phenomenon. As one who is compelled to make his observations from the outside, he was, however, scarcely in position to fathom its possibilities. He dealt with immigration as a part of the general westward movement, which indeed it was; but looking at the history of the great inland valley from a slightly different angle, one seems to find that there were two separate movements heading into the West, one from across the mountains and another from over the sea. While the aim and the direction were the same in both streams, they seem to have flowed in distinct channels. For a long time the second movement was of little apparent consequence: except in the economic field it scarcely affected the current of American life and growth. The native element was and continued to be in almost complete control of all the great forces that were shaping the national destiny.

Time came, however, when the energies of the older

migration had begun to wane. The continent had been crossed; the West had been settled and organized. The work of the pioneer from the seaboard states had been pretty well completed by the close of the 1890's. Meanwhile, new energies had been brought into play. Strange names were appearing on the roster of achievement, names that were not British in any form. It is therefore not strange that many citizens of the older stock found the new situation disturbing and even menacing.

There are several important alien groups that may be used to illustrate the terms of the general problem of immigration, but the most convenient illustration is provided by that which came from Norway. Nearly all our foreign contingents are widely distributed throughout the nation and their activities are therefore lacking in effective unity. But the pioneers from the North have settled in large numbers within a limited area and thus form a fairly compact unit which, consequently, can be studied more effectively than any other immigrant group.

The first Norwegian settlement in the United States was formed in the autumn of 1825 when a group of about fifty men and women established homes at Kendall, New York, some thirty miles northwest of Rochester. A site on a great lake would seem to have its advantages; but the ground was difficult to clear, and the settlers soon began to ponder the advisability of seeking a new location.

So in 1833 Cleng Peerson, who had selected the site at Kendall, went forth again in search of the land of ease and plenty. Traveling on foot through Michigan, Wisconsin, and Illinois, he visited many promising locations and finally found what he sought in the Fox River Valley, about sixty miles southwest of a little forlorn village called Chicago. So convincing was Peerson's report that the settlers at Kendall promptly began to make preparations for a trek into the West. The following spring six men, all heads of families, followed the restless scout to La Salle County, Illinois,

where as soon as possible they purchased land and built
homes. Others came later and for some years the bulk of
such immigration as there was from the North was directed
toward Illinois.

Heading northwestward to spy out the land, some of
these newcomers found their way into the beautiful valley
of the Rock River. Soon the stream of settlement began
to flow northward toward the upper stretches of this valley
in southern Wisconsin, where lakes and streams, prairies
and woodland promised an abundant life. This was in 1838.
Two years later a settlement was formed near Lake Koshkonong, about twenty miles southeast of Madison. Though
there were many other favored places, this colony soon developed a great interest as the leading point of dispersion.
Immigrants in considerable numbers would go to Koshkonong, remain there for a time with friends or kinsmen,
and would then move on to newer fields.

Early in the forties the tide of Norwegian migration began
a steady progress westward and northwestward toward the
great river. Late in the decade it reached the counties of
northeastern Iowa. In the early fifties it touched various
points in eastern and southern Minnesota. Norwegian
settlers appeared in Dakota in 1859; but real settlement in
that territory did not come till the close of another decade.

The Civil War served to discourage emigration in every
land, Norway with the rest, though some venturesome souls
risked the journey over the sea even in those perilous days.
At the close of the war activities in the steerage took on new
life. Only 298 immigrants had arrived from Norway in
1860. In 1866 the number rose to 12,633, approximately
three-fourths of one per cent of the entire population of the
kingdom.

These new arrivals went to many parts of the country;
but the largest number came with the intention of establishing homes in the wheat lands of Minnesota. In the seventies
James J. Hill began to apply his amazing energies to the

problem of a transportation system for the Red River Valley. Next he initiated an active and widespread propaganda, especially among the newer Americans, calling their attention to this wonderful land "where the depth of the humus was equal to the height of a man." The Northmen responded with enthusiasm. In the twelve counties that border on the Red River at least one-third of the population is of Norwegian stock.

Thus there was formed, in the half century following Cleng Peerson's visit to the Fox River country, a geographical unit which has sometimes been called the "New Norway." This area extends from Lake Michigan westward into the Dakotas and well on toward the Missouri River, or to the margin of the land with insufficient rainfall. A somewhat irregular line drawn westward from Chicago to Sioux City will approximately mark the southern boundary. The area thus delimited will include half a dozen counties in northeastern Illinois, a dozen counties in northern and central Iowa, nearly all of Wisconsin and Minnesota, and the eastern parts of the two Dakotas, approximately one-third in either case. Within these boundaries eighty per cent, and possibly more, of all the Norwegians who have come to the United States have found their homes. To a great extent their descendants still have their homes in this region. Their number is variously given, but a million and a quarter, or possibly a million and a half, seems to be a conservative estimate.

It is not to be understood that this element is in actual majority in any large part of this area. Winnebago County in northern Iowa has a population which is probably four-fifths Norwegian; but this condition must be regarded as exceptional. The important fact is that the Northwest has been settled by many racial elements and that among these the Norse contingent is one of the more numerous; in many localities it is the most numerous. Its actual strength is therefore greater than its numbers would seem to indicate.

Our naturalized citizens usually have much to say about a heritage which they have brought to the New World and which it is their duty to defend and maintain. When pressed for details as to what this heritage really is, they usually point to the achievements of the past. But the past cannot very well be transplanted, and what is transplanted does not always thrive. Heritages that are worth while are those qualities of body, mind, and spirit which through millenniums of development in a stubborn environment have become part of the national self. The heritage of the alien is those powers and qualities and tendencies that determine what he is, what he is able to do, and what he is likely to do in the new surroundings.

The great novelist Arne Garborg, whose home was in the coast country of southwestern Norway, has described his neighbors in the following trenchant sentence, "They are a strong, stubborn folk who dig their way through a life of brooding and care, putter with the soil and search the Scriptures, force a little corn from the earth and hopes from their dreams, put their faith in the penny and trust in God." The picture is striking rather than attractive; but after all, such men were built for pioneering.

The Norwegian immigrant came with a strong attachment to the soil. He hungered for land; he felt the need of a home. A home, however, could not be a mere abiding place: home, as he saw it, was something to which one has the title of ownership. In his attitude toward society he was often stubbornly individualistic. It was his great pride that he came from a land of democratic freedom. In his quiet, somewhat unemotional way he was deeply religious. In the Lutheran faith he had found a religion that brought responses from his inner being; he was a strenuous defender of the traditional faith. In the homeland he had frequently acted in opposition to his superiors; but he usually believed in yielding obedience to law. Finally, like most aliens, he suffered from a troublesome suspicion of inferiority, and to disguise this he spoke freely and sometimes boastfully of his fatherland and of its glorious past.

He discovered early in his sojourn in the West that he was being exploited by the native element. Too often the banker, the lawyer, the wheat buyer, and other "smart" business men coined good money from his ignorance of American ways. For his economic protection, therefore, he realized that he must settle among men of his own race; he felt that he was safer among his own countrymen, and in this he was usually correct.

There were other and more weighty reasons why large alien settlements were inevitable. "It is hard to live among strangers," especially among strangers whose life and language one does not understand. Under such conditions there can be no active spiritual life. So there grew up several hundred communities where the whole intellectual civilization was in many respects quite foreign to normal American life.

In this connection one should note the significant fact that these settlements were flanked by hundreds of other alien communities inhabited by Swedes and Danes and Germans. In Minnesota the Swedes are as numerous as the Norwegians; in Wisconsin the Germans are by far the strongest alien element, the Norwegians holding second place. As for northern Illinois, one may recall the remark of a famous mayor that Chicago was the sixth largest German city in the world. In the 1890's a young man advertising for employment in that city closed his advertisement with the enlightening sentence, "Can speak both languages."

It is scarcely necessary to observe that Germans and Scandinavians belong to kindred branches of the great Germanic stem and in large part profess the Lutheran faith. The influence of Protestant Germany has been powerful all through the North. The Lutheran church gave its adherents not only a religion but a philosophy of life. The men and women who came into the West from the Atlantic seaboard were also largely of Germanic blood; but their religious background was Calvinistic. The older Calvinist was a child of God in a very intimate sense, one whose life was constantly being shaped and directed by an overruling Providence. The Lutheran, too, is a man of intense religious convictions; but his ideas as to the demands of the Almighty are not exactly the same as those of his Reformed brother. Lutheran ethics seems to allow a greater freedom to the individual conscience than the Calvinistic system appears to grant. It is true that these differing views of life are no longer so clearly marked as they once were; but such trends of change as one can observe appear to be moving away from the Reformed point of view.

Today the strongest single church in the area under consideration is the Roman Catholic. But among the Protestants the Lutheran organizations have the largest following. In the four states of Minnesota, Wisconsin, and the two Dakotas (taken as a unit) more than two-thirds of the entire Protestant membership is enrolled in Lutheran churches.

Soon after settlement came organization, first of all parochial organization, for the church was the chief unit in the system of defenses which were erected to stem the advance of an unfamiliar and possibly hostile culture. Church organization among the Norwegians in the West dates from 1843, when sixty-nine farmers in Muskego, Wisconsin, joined in a move to secure a pastor. Today, after ninety years, this group of sixty-nine has grown into a powerful body of churches with a membership of more than half a million.[1]

Next in point of time came the foreign-language newspaper. The first Norwegian newspaper was a little sheet with a Free-Soil program which began publication in 1847 in a log house in Muskego. Since then more than five hundred periodicals of various sorts have seen the light; but the rate of mortality has been high and most of them have ceased to

[1] A letter from the secretariat of the church dated January 15, 1934, gives the number as 491,957, children included. To this number should be added an associate membership of 77,328.

be. It is evident that the foreign-language press has done much to foster an alien culture on American soil; but it has also done much to familiarize the naturalized citizen with the institutions and the public life of the land.

The belief that the culture of the Northland would be able to take firm root in western soil was general in the Norwegian settlements in the decade following the Civil War. It had strong adherents even as late as the 1890's, though many had by that time come to understand that the earlier views were no longer tenable. But the tide of immigration was still pouring into our Atlantic ports; the older settlements were growing in strength; new ones were being constantly formed. A strong sense of power had entered into the souls of those to whom the rank and file looked for leadership. This found expression in part in the founding of higher schools, some of which have attained collegiate rank. During the nineties fifteen such institutions were established. The laws and rules of these foundations show clearly that the immigrant mind was moving toward a differing point of view. The new institutions were to be American in every respect; but the language and the culture of the motherland were to have the seats of honor at the new tables and were to be made subjects of serious study and cultivation.

Norsedom is still a virile force in the Northwest, though the program of the nineties, like that of the seventies, has proved a failure. New interests have come into the lives of the immigrant children, interests which threaten to smother those to which they were born. The greatest of all these disintegrating forces is intermarriage. In the seventies, if a man sought a wife outside his nationality, he was guilty of a form of disloyalty that could scarcely be forgiven. Marriage with other Scandinavians was, of course, always a proper proceeding; a German bride, too, might expect to be blessed, if she was of the right congregation. Further the leaders would not go. But the primal urge proved too powerful even for a hostile opinion. As many as forty per cent of Norwegian marriages are now contracted beyond the pale.

Then came the World War. Superpatriots clamored for the removal of foreign symbols of every sort. Churches using foreign languages were closed by orders from the state capitol. Many militant citizens tried to divest themselves of all the inherited garments that their souls could spare. A body blow was delivered by the immigration act of 1921, which dried up the sources from which the settlements had renewed their strength.

The depression followed. Even a dull imagination can see what the present economic misery must have done to colleges, academies, newspapers, and publishing houses. The walls that seemed so strong to the generation of the seventies and even to that of the nineties are badly shattered. The old language has practically passed out of the Norwegian Sunday schools and is rapidly being displaced as the language of worship in the urban churches. In the Norwegian Lutheran church two-thirds of the church services are now carried out in the English language.

On the positive side there are certain attractions in American life which to many have proved irresistible. As the young men and women became better acquainted with the system within which they moved, they found much which they wished to make their own. This might mean that they would have to desert the leadership of the elders. After a time Norwegian names began to appear in business, in academic life, and in many other fields. But the field into which the new urge led most directly was politics.

The Norwegian immigrant loyally accepted the political system of the new homeland. He applied early for naturalization; he took pride in his new citizenship. Before 1850 he felt drawn toward the Democratic party; but the great conflict over union and slavery brought him and his fellows into the Republican haven, where most of them remained for half a century and even longer.

The Norseman is by nature a politician. In the gray dawn of Northern history he appears as a sovereign freeman with a full share in the management of local concerns. Even in the long Danish period he did not entirely lose his political rights. In those dull days he often made life a misery to the priests and judges, bailiffs and tax collectors who came into his parish with credentials from the king's own Copenhagen. His descendants came to the West with a training which has not been allowed to grow stale.

In 1839 a Norwegian settlement was formed near Muskego Lake some twenty miles southwest of Milwaukee. The location proved to be unfortunate; soon there was much distress in the colony. The Whig leaders at the county seat organized the settlement into a township a few years later in order that the aliens might be forced to carry on their own relief work. Similar situations arose in many other places and the new citizens were called on to fill local offices even before they were really prepared to do so. It was not long before alien representatives appeared in the court-houses, and as the years passed an occasional Norseman would find his way into higher office; but one suspects that frequently the deciding factor in such cases was membership in the Grand Army of the Republic. H. B. Warner, who was elected secretary of state of Wisconsin in 1875, had credentials from Libby Prison.

The first great political clash between Norse and native leadership came in 1882, when Knute Nelson was put forward as a candidate for Congress in western Minnesota. After a bitter fight the Republican convention divided and two candidates were nominated. The campaign was animated and stirred racial feelings on both sides. Nelson was elected. He died forty years later as a member of the United States Senate. In those same years another Norwegian, Adolph Bierman, was coming forward as a leader in the Democratic party. Bierman was not always elected but he had amazing success as a vote-getter.

Clan feeling has to a great extent passed away. Still, there are many localities where a foreign name continues to be a political asset. Of the county officials listed in the current *Minnesota Year Book* about one-third bear Scandinavian names. In about a dozen counties the number is more than half the total; in one instance (Norman County) seventeen of the eighteen appear to be Scandinavians, all Norwegians but one.

Other nationalities can show a similar though less emphatic record. In Chisago County, where the Swedes are in control, only four, possibly only two native Americans appear to hold office in the courthouse (McLean and McGuire are counted among the Americans). The Swedes seem further to have appropriated the three members of the legislature from the Chisago district. The radio reports from Minnesota on election night in 1932 sounded like a roll call in the steerage.

Since the Norwegian element in America scarcely amounts to more than one and one-half per cent of the total white population it can scarcely expect to have more than half a dozen members in the national Congress. In the Congress that expired last March the number was actually thirteen. In the sad occurrences of 1932 several of these lost their membership. Minnesota, however, elected five Norwegians to the present House of Representatives. Of the remaining four, two seem to be Swedes.

Along with aggressiveness at the ballot box the Norwegian-Americans have in later years shown an emphatic independence in voting. This is particularly true in the newer settlements. Many Norsemen went into the Populist movement some forty years ago. They counted heavily in the La Follette following in Wisconsin and the neighboring states. They have come to be a powerful element in the Farmer-Labor movement in Minnesota. Elsewhere, too, they have shown serious symptoms of radical thought.

Grand Forks County, North Dakota, where nearly one-half of the voting population is Norwegian, offers an excellent illustration of independent or, if one prefers, erratic voting. The county began to vote for president in 1892, and though it has always had a somewhat restless electorate, the Republicans managed to secure majorities for their candidates from Harrison to Taft. Trouble began in 1912. In that year Wilson carried the county, Roosevelt following close behind. Wilson won again in 1916. Since that year Grand Forks County has given majorities to Harding, La Follette, Hoover, and Roosevelt. This is a record that is not easily matched.

There should be no need of an extended argument to show that the presence in the Northwest of a numerous and aggressive element like the Norwegian group must have been a powerful influence in the development of that region. One may go further and say that similar results are sure to appear in any section that has received an important immigrant population. It is true that the immigrant is becoming an American; but this statement is not very helpful, since there seems to be no agreement as to what the term American may imply. The naturalized citizen has indeed accepted the language and the institutions of the land, though frequently without having mastered either. He has further accepted the more important elements of American culture. Still, there are notions, principles, implications, and national habits which he has often been very reluctant to accept. Furthermore, he has brought with him a culture of his own, certain elements of which he is very reluctant to discard. Thus there is going forward throughout the American North a clash of ideas and principles, a conflict of mental habits and modes of thought which is likely to result in significant changes in the deeper strata of American thought.

It seems reasonable to assume that when these many and diverse alien strands have been thoroughly woven into the web of our national life, the pattern is likely to suffer many changes.   Perhaps one may even be allowed to raise the question whether this mingling of peoples will not also eventuate into a new physical type, or possibly more than one. The original American stock still flourishes in comparative purity in the South, where there has been only slight immigration except from the northern states.   In the South, too, the churches are mainly Protestant of British origin. There, too, one is likely to encounter what still remains valid of the Calvinistic view of life.

Wholly different is the situation in New England.   There is still much Puritan stock in the land but it now forms a thin layer stretching across the continent from Salem to Salem, from Portland to Portland.   Into the land of Cotton Mather and Jonathan Edwards have come the Irishman and the Italian, bringing a hostile religion and a differing view of life.   And no one can predict the racial future of Manhattan with its many tributary cities where all races have gathered, including powerful elements from the island of Sicily and from the great European Jewries.   In the Northwest the problem is relatively simple.   All the chief ingredients of the population, British, German, and Scandinavian, are fundamentally Germanic. The fusion in this area will inevitably produce a Germanic type, though in some of its prominent characteristics this may differ somewhat from the older types that we think of as essentially Teutonic.

The historian cannot, of course, be concerned with the years that are yet to come, but in his own proper field his duty lies clear before him: these alien contingents in our population must all be made the subject of serious and intensive study.   That such a program presents great difficulties, especially in the matter of linguistic preparation, will be evident without further discussion.   The historical profession has long been aware of the fact that research in certain fields and subjects of Old World history may demand special and even extensive preparation.   With the coming of so much of the Old World to our own shores the same condition has appeared in our own historical work.

Only recently has it become possible to carry on satisfactory research in the history of the naturalized groups. The chief difficulty in the past was the great poverty of available materials. This condition is now being rapidly remedied. The last two generations have been gathering into college libraries, the archives of historical societies, and other depositories important documentary collections in languages other than English. In this connection mention may be made of the activities of the Norwegian American Historical Association, which for some years has sponsored a search for pertinent historical materials on both sides of the sea.

One of the most interesting exhibits in the Illinois library is a collection of foreign-language newspapers, published chiefly in the great industrial centers of the Northeast and the Middle West. No doubt there are similar collections in other libraries, though there is probably none more complete for recent years than the one on the Illinois campus. The work of collecting materials of this sort in a large way was begun by Professor P. L. Windsor, the librarian, some twenty years ago and has been continued to date. The titles at present number 281; and, though many have not been able to survive the "depression," the number of papers received each week is still large. Almost every important European language and some Oriental idioms are represented on the shelves: Albanian, Arabic, Armenian, Hungarian, Lithuanian, Ukranian, Yiddish, and many more, thirty-one in all at the last count. Each of these files contains materials for a distinct chapter of our national history; and these chapters must all be written, if the complete story of American achievement is to be told.

On the coast of southern Norway, not far from the point where the more placid waters of Larvik Fjord join those of the restless and moody Skagerrack, lies Fredriksværn, a little town of about fifteen hundred inhabitants, which has for some time been known as a place where one can spend a delightful vacation period in spring or summer. Ninety years ago it was an important naval station and was also the seat of an academy where young Norsemen were instructed in the science and art of navigation. This institution is no longer in Fredriksværn, having been moved to the larger borough of Horten on the upper stretches of Oslo Fjord; but as a naval station the little town is still somewhat important.

To citizens of another land Fredriksværn has an interest only as the birthplace of Hjalmar Hjorth Boyesen, a Norwegian immigrant to the United States who was able to win for himself a high place in the field of American literature. From the point of view of Norwegian history in the New World, this achievement is unique as well as significant. For Boyesen was the first writer of Norwegian birth or blood to use the English language in the successful cultivation of literary art. Others may have tried to achieve a similar success in earlier years; but of such attempts the writer has found no record. Boyesen, however, used English and used it effectively, almost from the very outset of his literary career. With his arrival in the West in 1869 we date the beginning of a new chapter in the intellectual history of the Norwegian people in the United States. Moreover, the Boyesen name is not only the first but remains the most prominent one throughout a large part of the chapter.

The story of Boyesen's migration to the United States begins with Captain Sarolf Fredrik Boyesen, who in the 1840's held a commission in the Norwegian army. His duties were, however, not distinctly military; actually he was employed in the navy, having been appointed to an instructorship in the academy at Fredriksværn. In the early fifties, apparently in 1851, he was transferred to Kongsberg, where he remained only a few years. His career in the army was nearing its close, for he and his family had embraced the teachings of the great Swedish philosopher-mystic, Emanuel Swedenborg. In our time a change of religion would not interfere with military promotion; but in those days such a move could lead to no other result. The servants of the state were all expected to give their undivided allegiance to the established church.[1]

The young captain had taken as wife Helga Tveten Hjorth, whose father held a judicial appointment in the territory of Sogn.[2] Of the earlier history of the Hjorths and the Boyesens the writer has been able to learn almost nothing; the names, however, are significant and seem to justify the belief that, like so many other families of the upper or so-called "conditioned" class, they may have had an older history in Denmark.

On the twenty-third day of September, 1848, there was born in the Boyesen household a son who was given the name Hjalmar Hjorth. The first six years of his life the little boy spent with his family in Fredriksværn and Kongsberg. In 1854 Captain Boyesen left Norway and remained abroad for nearly two years. These years his family spent

[1] Sarolf Boyesen was the son of Peter Boyesen, who owned a large estate, Hovind, near Oslo. The future captain was born at Hovind on September 1, 1817. His mother was Helga Tullberg, the daughter of a merchant in Oslo. In 1876 Captain Boyesen emigrated to America and located in Vineland, New Jersey, where he died October 5, 1894. His death is noted in *Vineland Historical Magazine*, 21:373 (July, 1936), where the date of his birth is given (no doubt erroneously) as October 12, 1820. For these and other details relating to the Boyesen family the author is indebted to Miss Austa Boyesen, a sister of Hjalmar Hjorth Boyesen. For a useful printed account of the Boyesen kindred see an article by F. E. Heath in *Scribner's Monthly*, 14:776 ff. (October, 1877).

[2] Helga Helene Tveten was the daughter of an organist, Tveten, but was adopted by Judge Hjorth, who was a relative of the Tveten family. She died in 1859 at the age of thirty-one. This information was provided by Austa Boyesen.

at Systrand at the home of his father-in-law, Judge Hjorth. When Hjalmar was still a child of about eleven his mother died and the boy passed definitely into the care of his grandparents in the West Country.[3]

Systrand is a strip of shoreland in Mid-Sogn on the north side of the great fjord. The Sogn country is famous for its wild, impressive, overwhelming scenery; in this respect the new surroundings differed widely from the more serene and generally cheerful lowlands in the Larvik area. For eight or nine years Hjalmar passed a great part of his time with his grandparents at Systrand. These years must have meant a great deal to the future author. Boyesen was to win laurels in poetry as well as in prose; and one may safely affirm that the education of the poet began when Hjalmar came to live on his grandfather's farm.

One can rest assured that the tutors at Systrand did not neglect the conventional subjects of study; still, one is inclined to believe that young Hjalmar learned more outside the classroom than from his formal exercises inside. What he learned most readily was the weird lore of the old and the wise among the rural folk, who knew so well and could tell so vividly what was going on in the invisible world that lay all about them: the world of trolls and giants, of nixes and hulders, and of all those other nether-world beings who had their abode in springs and lakes and mountainsides and sometimes even in roaring waterfalls and towering trees.

Norwegian folklore is of ancient origin; in large part it is a heritage from heathen times. At present it is of scarcely more than antiquarian interest; but three generations ago it still retained much of its old vitality as a part of rural culture. In the quarters occupied by the serving folk on the Hjorth estate, tales and legends were apparently a regular form of entertainment. There the young boy experienced many an awesome thrill. It is told that his grandmother did not wish him to consort with the servants, possibly for

[3] *Scribner's Monthly,* 14:777.

reasons of class consideration; but her grandson was not always obedient. If he thought that there might be stories to hear, he would often steal down the dark stairs to the barn, or the bakehouse, or wherever it was that the workers congregated for a social hour at the close of day.

After a year in this environment, Hjalmar began to believe that he was called to be a poet. On his twelfth birthday he received a copy of Tegner's romantic poem *Frithiofs saga,* the scene of which was laid in the Mid-Sogn area.[4] It is likely that this gift proved an important influence in the young boy's life. At any rate his muse was now busying itself largely with heroic materials. Some of the more fearsome tales that were current in the neighborhood were speedily turned into verse.

When he was fifteen his interest turned to the drama and he began to experiment with tragic themes. Thus far his literary activities had been his own deep secret; but now he shared it with his grandmother "and was much encouraged by her tears which flowed with gratifying copiousness" when the lines were particularly moving and tragic. When he had reached his sixteenth year he laid his work and his ambitions before his father. This time, however, he received no encouragement. The writer's profession was one that no Boyesen could afford to choose. Poetry was a luxury which the wealthy alone were able to buy, and Norway was a land of little wealth.[5]

When Hjalmar was ready for secondary school work, his grandfather sent him to the Latin school in Drammen. Later the boy spent some time in the gymnasium in Christiania. From the gymnasium he passed quite naturally to the liberal arts department of the national university. In Drammen and Christiania he was two hundred miles or more from his home at Systrand. The ancient roadways crawled north-

---

[4] H. H. Boyesen, *Essays on Scandinavian Literature,* 260 (New York, 1895).
[5] See an article by Boyesen in the *Indianapolis News,* September 30, 1893. See also *Scribner's Monthly,* 14:778.

westward up through narrow dales and over the crest of the Norwegian plateau, which in some stretches is Arctic in all its important forms of life. But the difficulties of the highway did not deter the young student. When the academic year had reached its close, young Boyesen, with a few jovial friends from the classroom, would sometimes set forth with scrip and staff to cover the distances on foot.[6] The routine of study had closed; but in these journeys through a constantly changing landscape, lovely, barren, enchanting, and austere, the education of the scald was resumed.

Boyesen finished his course at the university in 1868. He was then a few weeks short of twenty years old. The question now was: what was his life work to be? He was still ambitious to be a writer, but the paternal will continued adamant in its opposition. Once more his father argued that the rewards of literature were sure to be insignificant, since Norway already had a larger number of writers than the reading public was able to support. Of course, if Hjalmar could achieve a mastery of one of the more widely used idioms, a mastery so complete as to enable him to write effectively in that language, that was a different matter.[7] This suggestion the young graduate did not forget. In later years he must have regarded it almost as a prophecy.

Since he had shown an unusual aptitude for language study, his friends advised him to make philology his professional subject. Once more the elder Boyesen interposed objections. There was no good reason, he believed, why a young man of twenty should be in a hurry to select a career. In a letter written at this time he urged his son to set forth to see what he could of the world before settling down to the routine of specialized study. It had been his own misfortune, the captain confided, "to wake up to experience the happiness of this broader and freer life only when it was too late to obey the impulse which it prompted." The part of the world which he was most anxious for his son to visit was

[6] *Scribner's Monthly*, 14:777.
[7] *Indianapolis News*, September 30, 1893.

America. He himself had traveled in that wonderful country and realized thoroughly the rich opportunities that it
had to offer.[8]

The old judge was, however, not disposed to regard this
suggestion with much favor; in fact it looked to him like
very bad advice. Norway was, in his mind, a good country,
and he saw no reason why a man of his grandson's training
and ability should not be able to have a successful, even
brilliant, career among his own people. As usual the discussion ended in a compromise. Hjalmar should have a year
abroad, but one year only.[9] The terms of the agreement are
not further recorded. Perhaps the understanding was that
monetary remittances were to cease at the end of the twelve
months. But whatever the arrangement, fate had decreed
that the young traveler was not to see his native land again
for several years — not till 1873, when he was allowed a few
days in and about the old haunts.

II

On the first day of April, 1869, Hjalmar Hjorth Boyesen,
accompanied by his younger brother Ingolf, landed in New
York.[10] In this city he was to spend the greater part of his
life in the New World. Here he was to attain high fame and
honors as a writer and teacher. But at that moment he
had no real interest in New York. His immediate destina-
tion was not the great metropolis but a little prairie town in
western Ohio.

After a few months of travel, chiefly in New England, the
two young immigrants "took up . . . temporary quarters in
a small town called Urbana." [11] Urbana, Ohio, was at the
time an important center of the Swedenborgian propaganda
in the West. It was the home of Urbana University, the

<hr />

[8] *Scribner's Monthly,* 14:777; *Indianapolis News,* September 30, 1893.
[9] *Scribner's Monthly,* 14:778.
[10] *Critic,* 27:237 (October 12, 1895); *Indianapolis News,* September 30, 1893.
The sketch in the *Critic* is anonymous but has been attributed to Boyesen's
friend and colleague, W. H. Carpenter.
[11] *Critic,* 27:237.

only institution maintained by the New Church west of the Appalachian Mountains. It will be recalled that the Boyesen family were Swedenborgians, and doubtless this is why the two young wanderers rested a while in Urbana; in other respects the drab little country town could have no attraction for them.

Boyesen did not at this time remain long in Ohio. Leaving his brother in the college town, he betook himself to Chicago, where he found employment on the editorial staff of *Fremad,* a Dano-Norwegian weekly newspaper which had been founded in Milwaukee in April, 1868.[12] In March, 1870, the publisher moved his paper to Chicago, and in the first number issued from the new offices (March 10) he informed his readers that he had added two university graduates to his editorial force: Hjalmar H. Boyesen of Christiania and P. G. Müller of Copenhagen, who was a knight of the Order of Dannebrog.

For a period of ten weeks the paper carried the names of its three editors, one of whom was the publisher, S. Beder. But in the issue of May 19 these names were absent and the omission became permanent. It may be that one of Beder's acquisitions, the knight of Dannebrog, did not prove a journalistic success. Some years later Boyesen published a story entitled *A Knight of Dannebrog,* in which he describes an inflated and impecunious knight who tried to be a newspaper reporter and failed, as he had in almost everything else that he had undertaken. It is probable that the author has given us a picture of his colleague, P. G. Müller.[13]

It seems to be generally believed that Boyesen in his editorials took a firm stand in defense of the public-school sys-

[12] When a writer in the *Critic,* 27:237, quotes Boyesen to the effect that he "was offered the editorship of a Norwegian weekly called *Fremad,*" he is manifestly inaccurate. It seems likely that Boyesen was a contributor to the paper in 1869, but he was not officially a member of the editorial staff before March 10, 1870. *Fremad* (Forward) was originally published by Just M. Caen, a Danish immigrant of the Hebrew race. In politics it was aggressively Democratic. The next year it passed into the hands of S. Beder, who was presumably also a Dane. Under his management *Fremad* became Republican.

[13] In *Ilka on the Hilltop and Other Stories* (1881).

tem and that he thereby incurred the ill will of the Norwegian Synod, the clerical leaders of which were urging the establishment of parochial schools. An examination of the files of *Fremad* does not seem to justify this belief. The paper did, indeed, stand definitely on the side of the common school and could not therefore be a partisan of the Synod. But Beder was a cautious editor and managed to keep the discussion of all serious questions on a high level.

The writer has been able to find only two editorial articles signed with Boyesen's initials.[14] In one of these the young editor of twenty-one years discusses the movement led by Susan B. Anthony and Elizabeth Cady Stanton, and gives unqualified adherence to the old conservative views. In neither of the two does he discuss the common school, though he may, of course, have contributed unsigned articles to the discussion that had raged for some years, notably in the columns of *Skandinaven.*

With Boyesen an important desideratum was to achieve an early Americanization. His countrymen, he believed, could have little influence in American life until they cordially accepted the culture of the land. He held that it was the duty of every citizen not only to learn the English language but also to use it in everyday speech. These ideas he seemed to have developed in the editorial office and he applied them to his own case as soon as he was able to do so. "From the day I set foot on American soil," he stated in 1877, " I have never spoken the Norwegian language, except when I have been forced to do so." [15] It may be that this statement is not entirely accurate, but it expresses a purpose that came early into his thinking and one that he realized at a remarkably early date.

In this position [*as associate editor of Fremad*] I remained for about a year and a half, but the ambition to write was strong in

---

[14] Copies of *Fremad* are scarce. The writer has used the files in the library of the Luther Theological Seminary in St. Paul.

[15] *Scribner's Monthly*, 14:778; *Indianapolis News*, September 30, 1893.

me and I soon saw that, if I were to make a reputation as a writer, I must master the English language. To this end it was necessary to abandon all Scandinavian associations. I resigned my editorship and accepted a position as tutor in Latin and Greek at Urbana University.[16]

The institution at Urbana was a venture that had been long in preparation. It began to receive students in 1853 and for some years enjoyed a moderate prosperity. Then came the Civil War, and the institution all but closed its doors. Work was resumed in the later sixties and the future began to look more promising. " In 1871 an endowment of $50,000 was raised, a college-bred faculty secured, and the number of students brought up to eighty-three." [17]

Boyesen seems to have entered upon his duties in Urbana in the autumn of 1870. His brother Ingolf was still in town and his brother Alf, who had come from Norway that same year, was also enrolled in the college.[18] The young tutor remained with the " university " for two years. He was not happy in Urbana. The institution was an experiment in New Church education, with which a man of Boyesen's training and background could have little sympathy. When the university was first opened, instruction was given in " the entire curriculum from the primary grades through the college." [19] The situation was much improved by 1870, but Urbana University never became anything better than a third-rate college.

[16] *Critic,* 27:237. The statement that he was in the editorial work for a year and a half cannot be quite accurate. He states in his article in the *Indianapolis News* that "the years 1869 and 1870 I spent in Chicago editing a Norwegian paper *Fremad."* I find no record of such a paper in Chicago in 1869 and the Milwaukee *Fremad,* as stated above, was not moved to Chicago before 1870. No doubt Boyesen was in Chicago during the closing months of 1869 and during the greater part of 1870; but that can mean very little more than a year. Before moving to Urbana he spent some weeks in Boston with an "elocutionist" who was introducing him to "the niceties of sound" in English speech. See the *Indianapolis News,* September 30, 1893.

[17] Marguerite Beck Block, *The New Church in the New World,* 180 (New York, 1932).

[18] Ingolf K. Boyesen later studied law and became a lawyer of prominence in Chicago. Alf Boyesen also studied law; he practiced his profession in St. Paul. See O. N. Nelson, *History of the Scandinavians in the United States,* 1:348-349 (Minneapolis, 1893).

[19] Block, *The New Church,* 180.

Twenty years after his departure from the little Ohio town, Boyesen published what has been called his "most virile novel," *The Mammon of Unrighteousness*.[20] The scene is laid in Torreyville, a university town of some pretensions. Not knowing how pitifully small everything was in Urbana, some reviewers promptly concluded that boss-ridden Torreyville was a replica of the country town in Ohio and that the timid professors were his own colleagues from the early seventies. It is no doubt true that memories from those early days may have been used in building up the story; but they are scarcely more than a very minor element. The novel is a study of types, most of which are peculiarly American; and fifty years ago these were found in the greatest abundance in Boyesen's own state.

In the summer of 1871 Boyesen made a journey to Boston in the hope of interesting a publisher in a manuscript that he had completed a few weeks earlier. He also wished to see Cambridge, and one day in July he made a visit to the Harvard library, a visit which was to change completely the current of his life. Professor Ezra Abbott, the assistant librarian, asked him to write his name in the visitors' book. Evidently the name interested him.

He asked about my nationality and, hearing that I was a Norseman, begged leave to make me acquainted with Professor Child, who just then was in need of a Norseman. Professor Child was sent for and arrived. He gave me Landstad's collection of Norwegian ballads and begged me to read and translate a number of passages which he had marked. He was then at work upon his great book on ballads, two volumes of which have now appeared. We spent the whole afternoon reading Norse ballads written in different dialects which were all familiar to me. When we parted Professor Child exclaimed: "You have a lot of valuable material in your possession. Why don't you make use of it? It would make an interesting article."[21]

Boyesen now informed the great scholar that he had already written something and that he had brought the manuscript with him. Professor Child, whose enthusiasm

[20] New York, 1891.
[21] *Book Buyer*, 3:343. See also *Indianapolis News*, September 30, 1893.

was evidently quite genuine, proceeded to arrange a dinner
to which he invited, among others, William Dean Howells,
who was on the staff of the *Atlantic Monthly*. After dinner
the guests heard Boyesen read a chapter from his novel
Gunnar. The audience asking for more, he read a second
chapter. Howells was impressed and invited the young author to be a guest at his home for a few days. There the
two went over the greater part of the manuscript and Howells
liked the story well enough to accept it for publication in his
journal, where, in a slightly revised form, it appeared two
years later.[22]

Boyesen's almost chance acquaintance with Professor
Child had opened the door to a real opportunity; it was also
to have a determining influence in his professional life. In
those days President Andrew D. White was building a
faculty for Cornell University, which had been established
under his leadership only half a dozen years earlier. On the
recommendation of Professor Child, it is believed, Dr. White
got in touch with the tutor in Urbana. The outcome was
that Boyesen was offered, and no doubt promptly accepted,
a position as assistant professor of northern languages, which
position he held until 1877.[23] In that year the title of professor of German was added to that which he already held;
and for three years he enjoyed the unique distinction of
holding a major and a minor rank at the same time.

In the earlier years of its history Cornell had a " special
faculty " of north European languages, including, curi-
ously enough, the courses in German.[24] This faculty was
under the direction of Professor Willard Fiske, a unique personality with a deep and abiding interest in Scandinavian
culture. He was no doubt glad to have as a colleague " the
enthusiastic and showy Norwegian " who had made such a

[22] *Book Buyer*, 3:343.
[23] Boyesen received his appointment in 1873.
[24] In 1874 this faculty was composed of the president, Dean Fiske, and
Professors H. H. Boyesen, W. T. Hewett, and Bela P. MacKoon. Bayard
Taylor was attached to the faculty as non-resident lecturer.

distinct impression on the Brahmins of Boston and Cambridge. Fiske and Boyesen became firm friends. In addition to what they had in common in professional respects, they had a common religious heritage, both having come from families that had accepted the religious philosophy of Emanuel Swedenborg. It should be added, however, that neither had much enthusiasm for the New Church. Fiske had already become a nonconformist and Boyesen a few years later found a spiritual haven in one of the old historic churches.[25]

The demand for work in the northern languages at Cornell was never very important. Fiske and his colleagues did indeed train several competent scholars in northern philology, men like William H. Carpenter and A. M. Reeves; but Professor Fiske was able to care for whatever classes there might be in Scandinavian subjects and Boyesen was therefore assigned to the department of German.[26]

To prepare himself more thoroughly for his classroom duties, the new professor was given part of a year's leave of absence for travel and study in the Old World. Accordingly, in June, 1873, he embarked for Europe and apparently proceeded to Norway. There he spent part of his time traveling with Bjørnson, who was touring the country in the interest of the radical propaganda.[27] Most of his leave he spent in Leipzig, where he heard lectures at the university.[28] What courses he chose to audit we do not know, but his subjects of chief interest must have been philology and literature, perhaps with emphasis on the latter subject.

On his return journey, Boyesen visited France and England. His sojourn in Paris, brief though it doubtless was, proved to be a significant milestone in his literary career;

[25] Horatio S. White, *Willard Fiske*, 13, 14, 57 (New York, 1925).

[26] "Furthermore, instruction in Swedish was quite regularly given throughout the decade and also occasionally in Icelandic." White, *Willard Fiske*, 60-61.

[27] "I had the pleasure of accompanying Bjørnson on his first political tour in the summer of 1873, and I shall never forget the tremendous impression of the man and his mighty eloquence at the great folk-meeting at Bøe in Gudbrandsdalen." Boyesen, *Essays on Scandinavian Literature*, 48.

[28] *Galaxy* (New York), 17:456 ff.

for in that city he met the great Turgenev, who was just then at the zenith of his fame.   Armed with a letter of introduction from Dr. Julian Schmidt, a distinguished German student of literature in its historical aspects, he sought out the Russian exile and won his friendship almost at once. Boyesen was artistic in his tastes and at the time was toying with the idea of trying his hand as an art critic.   It has been stated that the two men visited the art collections for which Paris is famous, but that is quite unlikely.   That art was a leading subject in their conversation is, however, quite evident; and Boyesen returned to America with a set of novel ideas as to the inner nature of art, particularly literary art.[29]

In January, 1874, he appeared at Cornell to give instruction in German.   The lovely surroundings of Ithaca must have been a great relief from the drab littleness of Urbana. From his lecture room in South Building he had a wonderful view over Cayuga Lake, a view that a poet could not fail to enjoy.   On the wall he had hung several photographs of paintings of some of the greater men in German literature; and with them, and the most prized of all, was a signed photograph of the great Russian realist who had so thoroughly upset his notions of literary art.[30]

One might think that the poet-professor would have found much happiness in Ithaca, but such was not wholly the case. He was poorly paid for what, he believed, was good work, and as this condition continued from year to year he came to believe that his talents were not appreciated by the university authorities.   In this he was entirely in error: salaries were inadequate everywhere in the institution for the simple reason that they had to be kept adjusted to an inadequate income.[31]

In 1880 Boyesen resigned his professorship, expecting to

[29] *Galaxy,* 17:456 ff.; Theodore Stanton, " Boyesen at Cornell University," in the *Open Court,* 10:4812-4813.

[30] Stanton, in the *Open Court,* 10:4813.   See also *Columbia University Bulletin,* no. 12, p. 46-47.

[31] The writer is in debt to George Lincoln Burr, professor emeritus at Cornell University, for significant information as to Boyesen's career at Cornell University.

give his energies to literature and journalism. After a year's experience as a literary free lance, however, he regretfully came to the conclusion that this move had been a mistake. A year before his death he wrote to a friend advising him not to surrender a safe and secure position as a teacher for the very uncertain chance of making a success in journalism, as he had done when he severed his connection with Cornell University.[32]

"I was very glad," he added, "to resume the professorial harness at Columbia in 1881." A tutorship in German had become vacant and Boyesen was given the position, with the rank of instructor. In reporting the appointment to the board of trustees, President Barnard added that since Boyesen was "a Dane by birth" he would be competent to continue the course in Danish. It is not recorded that he ever gave any work that might specifically be called Danish; but in his first year at Columbia he did give a course in Norwegian literature, in which, by the way, the lectures were given in Dano-Norwegian. The course was not popular, only two students entered the class, and it was probably not repeated for some time.[33]

After a year's probation Boyesen was promoted to the Gebhard professorship, a chair that was normally occupied by the major professor in the department. In recommending this promotion the president stated that he "actually gives the largest part of the instruction in German." He wrote in high praise of Boyesen's scholarship and called attention to the fact that "during the past winter he has delivered, on invitation, a course of critical lectures on the poetry of Goethe and Schiller before the Lowell Institute in Boston."[34] To have been invited to give the Lowell lectures was a distinction that the authorities of the college could not afford to ignore.

[32] *Dial*, 19:323. Boyesen's letter was dated May 29, 1894.
[33] Columbia College, *Annual Report of the President*, May 1, 1882, p. 68 (New York, [1882]); Daniel Kilham Dodge, "Hjalmar Hjorth Boyesen the Teacher," in *Bachelor of Arts*, 2:823.
[34] *Annual Report of the President*, May 1, 1882, p. 68.

In 1890 his title was changed to professor of German language and literature. His courses were, however, at least in his last years at Columbia, exclusively on the literary side of the subject. Though he had always been a keen and enthusiastic student of language, he was never able to develop more than a perfunctory interest in philological problems. These he was glad to leave to his colleague, Professor W. H. Carpenter, who came to Columbia two years after Boyesen's arrival and, like him, after an apprenticeship at Cornell.[35]

Boyesen did not pretend to scholarship of the conventional type. Even when he was conducting elementary classes in German he was likely to wander off into literary discussions. As one of his Cornell students has phrased it, " he made grammar secondary to the poetry of speech."[36] Similarly one of his earlier students at Columbia has written of Boyesen's lectures on Faust: "There was little textual criticism and a minimum of grammatical and philological explanation. But this exclusion gave so much more time for following the manifold direction of the poet's thoughts and applying them to the intellectual and social condition of the present time." [37]

Such a man could not be a successful drillmaster; but as an interpreter he could be illuminating and even brilliant. In his courses he strove to get to the heart of the subject before him, for there he would expect to find the central idea of the author's thinking. When he discovered a thought that had earlier eluded him, he was visibly stirred, for Boyesen was " a man of ideas." [38]

III

Soon after his interview with Boyesen in July, 1871, W. D. Howells sent him a copy of Hans Christian Andersen's travel

[35] *Critic*, 27:237; *Columbia University Bulletin*, no. 12, p. 47.
[36] *Open Court*, 10:4813.
[37] Dodge, in *Bachelor of Arts*, 2:822.
[38] W. H. C[arpenter] in *Columbia University Bulletin*, no. 12, p. 47-48. See also *Sewanee Review*, 4:302, and *Open Court*, 10:4813.

story, *A Poet's Bazaar,* to review for the *Atlantic.* The review was prepared and published in October of the same year. So far as the writer has been able to learn, this was the first contribution submitted by a man of Norwegian birth or blood that had been accepted by the editor of a journal of standing in the American literary world.[39]

As was usual in those days, the review was not signed; but only four months later it was followed by a poem, "A Norse Stev," which closed with the signature Hjalmar Hjorth Boyesen. The larger part of this poem appeared later in *Gunnar,* from the manuscript of which it had doubtless been taken. The following year Howells published two other poems by the young author, "The Bride of Torrisdale" and "Saint Olaf's Fountain." [40] A fourth poem, "The Ravens of Odin," appeared in June, 1874. In all these excepting the first the author retold ancient legendary tales that he may have heard in his early boyhood days in old Sogn.

In April, 1873, Boyesen published a short story entitled "A Norse Emigrant" in the *Milwaukee Monthly Magazine.* It was indeed a "short" story, since it required only three printed pages to complete what it had to tell. Two months later *Gunnar* began to appear as a serial in the *Atlantic.* At first thought it seems strange that William Dean Howells, the major prophet of American realism, should have accepted *Gunnar* for publication. However, in 1871 he had not yet been converted to the new literary faith; in fact, he had not yet seriously begun to write fiction. He was still chiefly an editor, looking, as editors must, for fresh and possibly novel materials. No doubt he saw perfectly that Boyesen's novel was a decidedly amateurish production; at the same time he could not help seeing that, even if the plot was somewhat worn and thin, the narrative was exceedingly well written and, what was more interesting,

[39] The *Atlantic Monthly* was at the time publishing articles, stories and poems by Longfellow, Whittier, E. C. Stedman, Celia Thaxter, Lucy Larcom, and others in the same class.

[40] *Atlantic Monthly,* 29:210-211 (February, 1872) and 31:159-162, 418-419 (February and April, 1873).

it took the reader into an environment which was wholly new to the readers of the *Atlantic Monthly*.

" Gunnar was written merely to express my homesickness and longing for my beautiful native land during the first and second years of my sojourn in the United States." This statement has been taken to mean that the story was composed amid the dreary surroundings of Urbana, "a featureless and monotonous little town of red brick and frame houses." No doubt the novel was put into final form in that place.

I walked up and down along the railway track outside of the town by the hour and wrestled in thought with the successive chapters of that first romance of mine, *Gunnar*. For it was distinctly a romance; and I confess that I even contemplated the possibility of writing it in recess.[41]

The author's words may, however, also be taken to mean that the story was written, in some part at least, in Chicago, the beauty and loveliness of which, in 1870, was probably not exactly overpowering. Furthermore, there are indications here and there in the novel that it may have been written partly in Norwegian and later turned into English. That again may mean that the writing was begun before Boyesen had gained the mastery of the new language; but in such matters it is, of course, easy to be mistaken.

Gunnar appeared in book form in 1874. It was received in the East with loud acclaim. A reviewer in the *Atlantic* had evidently read it with rising enthusiasm:

Among the works of fiction printed in the English language this year, there can hardly be any so remarkable in some aspects as the idyllic story which Mr. Boyesen tells us . . . [The author is a] Norwegian thinking and expressing himself in our tongue with a grace, simplicity, and force and a sense of its colors and harmonies which we should heartily praise in one native to it.[42]

The reviewer further notes the fact that " Mr. Boyesen's citizenship is as new as the last election " (1874). *Gunnar* was soon out of print. An eighth edition was published in 1895.

41 *Indianapolis News*, September 30, 1893; cf. *Book Buyer*, 3:343.
42 *Atlantic Monthly*, 34:624 (November, 1874).

In the Northwest, among Boyesen's countrymen, the acclaim was more subdued. The Norwegian reviewers thought they could see distinct traces of Bjørnson's art in the new novel. It cannot be denied that Boyesen was profoundly influenced by the great Norwegian author; still it would be a mistake to assert, as some critics actually did, that he was a clever imitator and nothing more.[43] For Boyesen was an artist none the less. He was a master of written speech and had the sort of imagination that can visualize all the essential details of a given situation. But his scenes and environments are never wholly imaginary. "It is impossible for me," he has written in one of his prefaces, "to write a novel without having a distinct and real topography in my mind."[44] In *Gunnar* the scene is laid in Mid-Sogn amid the much beloved haunts of old Systrand. One is therefore not surprised to find a consistency in topographical details, a consistency which is always characteristic of Boyesen's novels, even when the environment does not seem to provide all the needs of the plot.

In 1873, when Boyesen's friends were following the new serial in Howell's journal, the author was himself in Europe. His sojourn in Leipzig cannot have been long; but it was long enough to give him a clearer insight into some of the literary problems of the fatherland. As a romanticist he would naturally be interested in the origins and principles of the German romantic movement. Later, after his return to America, his studies in this subject were set in order and published in the *Atlantic,* to which he continued to be an almost regular contributor.

When Boyesen went to Leipzig he was still an adherent of the cult of romanticism, though his faith had been somewhat shaken by the study of Turgenev's great novel, *Smoke.*

[43] Erik L. Peterson, who was perhaps the most competent literary critic among the Norwegian-Americans of his day, admitted that some of Boyesen's scenes were reminiscent of Bjørnson, but held that what imitation there was was quite unimportant. See *Budstikken* (Minneapolis), December 21, 1880.

[44] Preface to the *Mammon of Unrighteousness.*

But the ideas and tendencies that he discovered in the writings of the romantic school must have surprised him and given him pause. Perhaps he could accept the new beliefs in the sovereignty of genius and in the identification of poetry with philosophy; but the pallid mysticism of Novalis, and Schlegel's demand for complete freedom, even within the marriage relation, could have no attraction for a man who, though somewhat critical of social conditions, was by no means ready to dispute the essential rightness of the social structure.

These ideas were discussed in the first of these essays, "Social Aspects of the German Romantic School." "Novalis and the Blue Flower," the second in the series, deals with the career and the writings of Friedrich von Hardenberg, who has been regarded as the patron saint of the romantic movement. The last of the three essays, which the author entitled "Literary Aspects of the Romantic School," is a study in which he tries to bring into a clear light the literary faith of these great Germans; at the same time his own credo was changing: he was becoming an adherent of the new school of realism.[45]

If his faith in the ideals of romanticism had been shaken in Leipzig, it received an even more severe jolt in Paris. From the time of his first interview with Turgenev he continued an ardent admirer of his Russian friend. In his room in the Cascadilla dormitory in Ithaca he had on his bookshelves a set of Turgenev's works complete to date, some in French and some in German.[46] A few of these were the gift of the author himself. A new, a mighty influence had come into the young professor's life.[47]

On Boyesen's return to the United States he was soon made aware of the fact that his literary friend, William

[45] *Atlantic Monthly*, 36:49 ff., 689 ff. (July and December, 1875); 37:607 ff. (May, 1876).

[46] *Open Court*, 10:4813.

[47] He prepared an account of "A Visit to Tourguéneff" which was published in the *Galaxy*, 17:456 ff. (April, 1874). He saw Turgenev again in 1879. *Critic*, 1:81–82 (March 26, 1881).

Dean Howells, was also drifting away from the old moorings. Against these newer forces the older influence of the genial Bjørnson could no longer maintain its ascendancy in Boyesen's literary thinking. For that matter, the famous Norwegian had also begun to venture into the newer fields. Before long Boyesen's genius was to desert the misty realms of legend and find new subjects in the study of contemporary life. Soon the devotee of Norwegian romance was devoting his strength " to the task of brushing away all illusions and painting life as sterile and unpicturesque as it is in its meanest, most commonplace conditions." [48]

The conversion to the new faith was not immediate; nor was the process completed without serious strains and stresses. The poet in Boyesen continued partial to romantic themes. But during the decade of the seventies he became deeply interested in the achievements and possibilities of science, and once more science proved to be a ruthless solvent of old views. Finally the poet, too, had to capitulate. In the writer's opinion one of Boyesen's finest efforts is the group of five sonnets that he calls " Evolution," in which he glorifies life and all the mighty forces that have shaped the abode of man. One of these sonnets was published in May, 1878. [49]

A notable product of the period of transition in Boyesen's literary life was his second novel, *A Norseman's Pilgrimage,* which he probably composed in Ithaca in 1874. [50] In some respects the *Pilgrimage* is distinctly autobiographical; at least the hero and the author have much the same background. Like Boyesen, Olaf Varberg was brought up in the house of a grandfather who had a judicial appointment in Sogn. "Not a hundred steps from his home stood King Bele's venerable tomb "; and it happens that the ancient king's grave was not far distant from the Hjorth estate at Systrand. Olaf's father had made it possible for him to

---

[48] *Library of the World's Best Literature,* 5:2273–2274.
[49] *Idylls of Norway and Other Poems,* 124 128; *Atlantic Monthly,* 41:565-567 (May, 1878).
[50] New York, 1875.

spend a year in America. As in Boyesen's case his grand-father was strongly opposed to his leaving Norway. But soon after graduation he emigrated and became an enthu-siastic American. Like Boyesen again, he revisited Europe after some years and spent a few months in Leipzig. Here he met Ruth Copley, a young woman from Boston, and the story was ready to begin.

Like Boyesen, Olaf Varberg was a poet who quite early in life developed aspirations in that direction. At the age of twelve he wrote poems which he read to his grandmother. One of these she wept over " for a whole day, and that he felt to be a great reward."

Again like the author, the lonesome hero yearned for the beauties of his native land, " and in this dreary solitude Olaf sought refuge from the world in his old talent, that of song." In this case, however, the product was a story. And that which he had undertaken " to ease an overburdened mind gradually grew under his hand." Ultimately it found a pub-lisher.[51]

In a novel where fact and fiction are woven together with only slight regard for plan or pattern, it is always difficult to determine which details may be accepted as factual. But since Boyesen always wrote with an actual setting in his mind, one may feel confident that the " white, stately man-sion . . . on the green slope, close to the water," was the resi-dence of Judge Hjorth. One can also be reasonably sure that when he describes the great drawing room with its heavy, red curtains, its strange tapestries, its long row of ancestral portraits, he is describing the room where his grandparents entertained their visitors and friends.[52]

Another novel which some critics have regarded as a

[51] The details cited above are from chapter 2.

[52] See p. 214, 219. The story is the wooing and winning of Ruth Copley, a daughter of old Boston. There is a belief in Boyesen's family that he was at this time engaged to a young woman of the Longfellow family, though not a mem-ber of the Cambridge poet's household. Boyesen's " Elegy on A. G. L." (dated December 15, 1876, and published in *Idylls of Norway*, 8–10) is believed to have been written in her honor. If these surmises are correct, Miss Longfellow may have been the original of Ruth Copley.

chapter from Boyesen's own experiences is *Falconberg,* which Scribner's brought out in 1879. The leading character in the story is Einar Finnsen Falconberg, the son of a highly self-centered but mediocre Norwegian bishop, who had destined Einar to official preferment in the church. A forged paper destroys the young man's chance to make a career in theology and he sees no escape from his difficulties except in flight to the New World. In his wanderings he comes to Pine Ridge, a Norwegian settlement in Minnesota, where his uncle, Marcus Falconberg, has a pastorate. Under the name of Einar Finnsen, the young immigrant makes a place for himself in the community, finally becoming editor of a new Republican organ, the *Citizen.* He forms a few close friendships, wins the love of a young woman of ability and character, and all seems to be well.

He has not been long in the settlement, however, before he incurs the ill will of his uncle, the local pastor. Marcus Falconberg is one of those inflated personalities who try to maintain their positions by domineering tactics. He has long been regarded as the orator ex officio at the annual Seventeenth-of-May celebrations; but this year the committee in charge chooses the young editor. That fact alone would be sufficient to stir the ecclesiastical ire, but worse is to come. In his address, Finnsen takes a position on the subject of Americanization which the pastor can regard only as the rankest heresy.

Here in this wondrous land a new and great people is being born; a new and great civilization, superior to any the world has ever seen, is in the process of formation. It would be a foolish and ineffectual labor if we were to try to preserve our nationality intact, if we were to cling to our inherited language and traditional prejudices, and endeavor to remain a small isolated tribe, forming no organic part of this great people with which our lot is cast.[58]

In the course of the ensuing conflict, the angry cleric discovers who Finnsen is, and when the editor refuses to come to heel, he informs the world of his nephew's crime. The

[58] Boyesen, *Falconberg,* 134 (chapter 10).

community is properly shocked, but the editor's friends gather about him, his betrothed is loyal, and the story ends on a happy note.

A reviewer who had evidently read the book without much understanding seemed to see in the new novel a study in race antagonism. " The contact of slow conservative farmers from Scandinavia with the bustle and stir of Anglo-Saxondom in its American phase cannot fail to offer picturesque situations and these Mr. Boyesen has liberally used." [54]

Unfortunately for this analysis, there are only two important American characters in the story, one an eccentric scholar with a Dutch name and the other an editor and politician of low principles and little character. The " stir and bustle " is chiefly evident in the Norwegian circle. Of racial antagonism there is scarcely a trace.

Boyesen had written the novel for a wholly different purpose. He wished to illustrate his belief that the Norwegian clergy, with their insistence on maintaining Norwegian culture, were impeding the development of the immigrants into normal American citizens. Furthermore, he wished to expose what he believed to be the essential viciousness of the priesthood, its hypocrisy, its bigotry, and its domineering instincts. And he therefore gives a character to Marcus Falconberg which must have been rare on this side of the sea.

One can readily understand that the book could not be received with much favor in the Norwegian settlements. It was generally regarded as a vicious caricature for which there could be no warrant or provocation. The author finally came forward with a reply to his critics in which he asserted that he had no intention to lampoon the immigrant citizen. What he had tried to do was to describe the conflict between " the spirit of liberty and ecclesiastical reaction." It was quite true that the bolt was directed against

[54] *Scribner's Monthly,* 18:472 (July, 1879).

the Norwegian Synod; but he believed that when one
looked into the facts the charges would be found to be very
mild. Falconberg was, after all, not half so ridiculous or
papal as certain pastors who shared leadership in the
Synod.[55]

Two years later he lifted his voice once more against the
" reactionary " clergy in the West. Bjørnstjerne Bjørnson
spent the winter of 1880–81 in the United States lecturing
to his countrymen in the Northwest. The great author was
never famous for tact. He had become a " freethinker," and,
though he did not come into the West on a mission of
propaganda, he was unable, perhaps unwilling, to keep his
newer ideas under cover. It was only to be expected that
the clergy would meet him with sword in hand and the expectation was not disappointed.

The anti-Bjørnson agitation irritated Boyesen, and he
poured forth his wrath in a letter to the *Critic*: " The clergy,
as usual the representatives of obscurantism and bigotry,
began a fierce and determined warfare upon him the moment
his arrival was announced." He was sure, however, that the
Bjørnson progress had been worth while; "he has roused to
thought the great priest-ridden masses in the Scandinavian
West." [56]

The novel *Falconberg* shows clearly that Boyesen was entirely out of touch with the situation in the pioneer states.
The conflict over the common school had died down by the
time the novel was written. The work served therefore more
as a historical statement than as effective propaganda. One
wonders whether the author realized that in this story he
was repeatedly guilty of hitting below the belt. Mean little
egotists like the Reverend Marcus Falconberg no doubt

[55] *Budstikken*, February 15, 1881. See also the issues of December 21 and 28,
1880 (sympathetic review of Boyesen's works by Erik L. Peterson), and February 1, 1881 (reply to Peterson by Ole O. Lien).

[56] *Critic*, 1:58 (March 12, 1881) and 10:225–226 (March 7, 1887). In the
latter article Boyesen speaks approvingly of Kristofer Janson's novel, *Præriens
saga*, " in which he depicts in striking colors the obscurantism and the spiritual
thralldom to which a majority of the Norse emigrants submit."

held pastorates in Norwegian settlements but they probably
did not keep them long. It is recorded that their congregations knew how to deal with them. Marcus Falconberg is
an individual; he is not a type.

A critic might also object to the choice of environment
within which the scene is laid. Lakes are common in Minnesota, but ravines and canyons are not. The setting seems
rather to belong in the " finger lake " district in New York.
These discrepancies do not, however, detract materially
from the interest of the story. There is more strength and
vigor in *Falconberg* than in any of Boyesen's earlier writings.

Sixty years ago there appeared the first in a series of
novels which make up what we may call Norwegian-
American literature. It was Tellef Grundysen's story of
Minnesota life, *Fra begge sider af havet.*[57] *Falconberg*, the
second in the series, was published two years later. Both
dealt with life among the Norwegian pioneers in Minnesota.
But though Boyesen was not the first in point of time to
deal with the problems of immigrant life, we can at least
say this much, that he was the first author of real distinction to enter this field.

Boyesen was young when he left Norway; he was only
midway in his twenty-first year. It seems clear, however,
that he had attained an intellectual maturity far beyond
his years. He had drunk deep from the springs of Norsedom,
and the riches, intellectual and emotional, that he had acquired in his native land he treasured carefully and used
effectively in his literary profession. In spite of the fact that
he had become wholly assimilated to the American intelli-
gentia, he remained to the end of his days something of a
Norseman.

It is therefore not at all strange that such a considerable
part of Boyesen's literary output is concerned with Norwegian themes. The three novels that have been discussed
are all Norwegian in content, either wholly or in part. His
Tales of Two Hemispheres is a group of six stories, all of

[57] See *ante,* p. 54 ff.

which are Norwegian or have Norwegian backgrounds.[58]
Other writings of the same class are *The Modern Vikings,* a
group of short stories depicting life and sport in the Northland; *Boyhood in Norway; Against Heavy Odds,* a volume
in which the author pays tribute to Norse heroism; and
Norseland Tales,[59] a collection that was published only a
year before his death. The best of his poetry will be found
in a little volume that he named *Idylls of Norway and Other
Poems.*[60] This list is far from being exhaustive; but it is
sufficient to show that his fondness for Norwegian motifs
continued throughout his career.

In 1886 Putnams brought out Boyesen's *Story of Norway*
as a volume in the *Story of the Nation* series. In this work
the romanticist had a final inning. The glamorous heroes
of the Viking Age receive far more attention than the more
commonplace actors of the modern stage. The book is consequently not outstanding as history; but it makes delightful reading and in the author's own day it enjoyed high
favor.

In the field of literary history Boyesen's writings have a
greater claim to serious consideration. Some of his essays
in German literature, particularly his studies in the lives and
works of Goethe and Schiller, are still read in college and
university classes.[61] Of an even higher quality are his studies
of the modern literature of his native land. As early as 1873
he published an important article on " Bjørnstjerne Bjørnson as a Dramatist." He was also watching the rising star
of Henrik Ibsen and published a " commentary " on Ibsen's
dramas in 1894.[62] This was followed by a series of *Essays on
Scandinavian Literature.*[63] The larger part of this work is

---

[58] Boston, 1876.
[59] New York, 1887, 1892, 1890, 1894, respectively.
[60] New York, 1882.
[61] *Goethe and Schiller, Their Lives and Works* (New York, 1879); *Biographical Introduction to Schiller's Works* (Philadelphia, 1883); *Biographical Introduction to Goethe's Works* (Philadelphia, 1885); *Essays on German Literature*
(New York, 1892).
[62] *North American Review,* 116.109–138 (January, 1873); *Commentary on
the Works of Henrik Ibsen* (London, 1894).
[63] New York, 1895.

devoted to the great Norwegian writers, Ibsen, Bjørnson, Kielland, and Lie; but Boyesen also discusses such diverse Danish writers as Hans Christian Andersen and Georg Brandes; his Swedish representative is the celebrated romanticist, Esaias Tegnér, whose influence Boyesen felt at a very early age. Attention has been called above to a course in Norwegian literature that he gave in his first year in Columbia; this was later broadened into a course in Scandinavian literature. He was scheduled to give such a course in the year of his death.

There has been no attempt in this paper to list everything that Boyesen wrote; some of his strongest productions have not even been mentioned. In twenty-one years he published twenty-four volumes: novels, collections of short stories, essays in literary criticism, poetry, and history. In addition he wrote a large number of articles and did a great deal of reviewing. The doors to all the important editorial offices in the land were open to him, and all the literary journals were glad to publish whatever came from his pen. When the first number of the *Cosmopolitan* came from the press, it was found that Boyesen had contributed a story and that it had the first place in the issue.

In appraising what he wrote, critics have not always been kind. He was not, some of them have thought, a good poet. A reviewer writing in 1883 expressed himself in these terms, "Still, we hardly think there is warrant in it [*Idylls of Norway*] for ranking Mr. Boyesen as anything more than a receptive mind, possessed of a true but not original poetic tendency, serving art with reverent hands and conscientiously."[64] It is quite true that Boyesen's lines are often lacking in poetic grace, but the same can be said of most poets. And among the heavier lines are some that are worthy of a real master. The reviewer quoted above is willing to grant that the five sonnets to "Evolution" are poetry of a high order. The present writer would second this opinion and would like

[64] *Atlantic Monthly*, 51:423 (March, 1883). For a somewhat similar appraisal see Benjamin W. Wells in *Sewanee Review*, 4:302 (May, 1896).

to add that in the sonnets to "Lillie" there are many lines that deserve unqualified praise.[65]

Boyesen's verse may be heavy, but it is often energetic at the same time. The quality of his poetry is quite well illustrated in "The Minstrel at Castle Garden."[66] The minstrel is a Norwegian violinist perched high on a heap of chests and pouring forth his changing mood on the quivering strings:

Through a maze of wildering discords, — *presto* and *prestissimo* —
Runs the bow — a wild *legato* rocking madly to and fro,
As if wrestled in the music, hope and longing, joy and woe.

Boyesen's prose is generally regarded as better than his verse. His stories are simple and direct; they hold the reader's attention, though they sometimes give the feeling of having been written in too great haste. This seems to be more generally true of his shorter stories than of his full-length novels. Boyesen evidently had his stories outlined to the closing episode, and when he began to write, his pen moved rapidly forward to the last line. With him the main thing was the story; and in his eagerness to tell the tale he rarely stopped to apply artistic touches. Perhaps, as a realist, he did not believe in doing so, since lavish embellishment is likely to dull the reader's sense of reality.

But if his tales have the appearance of lacking in finish, they are always wholesome. Rarely does Boyesen offend against good taste. Forty years ago his writings were widely read, and their popularity has not yet disappeared. A test of this popularity is the fact that they have also been read in other countries. There are translations of some of his more important works in German, Norwegian, Italian, and even in Russian.

IV

The first number of *McClure's Magazine* carries a series of six photographs taken in various periods of Boyesen's life, as student, as editor, and as professor.[67] Those of the mature

[65] In *Idylls of Norway*. Lillie was the poet's wife.
[66] First published in *Century Magazine*, 24:850–851 (October, 1882).
[67] Pages 22–23 (June, 1893).

stage show a strong face framed in a bushy, somewhat unruly beard. The eyes are those of a man who is honest and frank, perhaps cruelly frank. "Frankness was the atmosphere of his life," wrote a friendly critic shortly after his death. He adds, however, that Boyesen "was rarely blunt or curt." He describes him further as a self-centered individualist, who insisted on living his own life. At the same time he absolves him from the charge of egotism.[68] It is probably true that in his outlook on life he was inclined to be cynical. He was a born controversialist. His opinions were firmly based and he never shrank from the duty of defending them; nay, rather he rejoiced in the opportunity.

Another critic finds in his writings broad traces of "burly humor [and] deep but not very delicate sentiment." He finds his satire somewhat heavy and combative.[69] But sometimes again his satirical observations are almost delicious and even when they are ponderous they are effective.

The estimates of men who knew Boyesen chiefly from his books are, of course, quite likely to differ from those made by men who knew him as a friend or as a classroom teacher. One of his students at Cornell remembered him best for his self-control, his restraint, and his moderation.

Though a zealous Republican in politics, he is not a jingo; though a reformer, he is not a fanatic; though an independent thinker in religion, he is not an atheist; and in literature and art, while a worshipper of the beautiful, he is not a defender of artistic immorality.[70]

Boyesen has been described to us as a man of the more distinctly blond type. His curly beard was of a reddish color and made a good frame for a face that was always "glowing with health." He was not tall but was of a compact build, " deep-chested and broad-shouldered." [71] To the week of his death he had never known what might be

---

[68] George Merriam Hyde in the *Dial*, 19:323–324.
[69] Benjamin W. Wells in *Sewanee Review*, 4:303.
[70] Theodore Stanton in the *Open Court*, 10:4813.
[71] W. H. C[arpenter] in *Columbia University Bulletin*, no. 12, p. 46. Cf. *Book Buyer*, 12:557.

HJALMAR HJORTH BOYESEN

regarded as serious illness. Such a man could not help being energetic even in his verse. His writings are the expression of a vigorous personality, and his literary style quite naturally partakes of a muscular quality. In his battle with the trolls of life he preferred the club to the rapier.

At the same time there was nothing repellent in Boyesen's attitude toward the world. He formed close friendships, and in his domestic relations he was thoughtful and considerate even to the point of tenderness. As a close observer of social conditions, he saw much to rectify, and he satirized human folly freely and in a certain biting manner which was effective even if not always enjoyable. But his work for reform did not stop with his labors in the study; as a citizen he knew his duties and was anxious to be helpful wherever practical measures were being proposed and promoted.

Like most Norwegian immigrants he early became a member of the Republican party. In the eighties, however, he was attracted to the sturdy personality of Grover Cleveland and soon became an enthusiastic Democrat. He even made a few speeches in the interest of Cleveland's candidacy for the presidential office.[72] It was characteristic of the man, however, always to reserve a freedom of action in all his public affiliations; and this attitude kept him from becoming closely identified with any political group.

When he emigrated Boyesen was presumably a loyal adherent of the religious philosophy of Emanuel Swedenborg, though one may doubt that he was very ardent in his adherence. During his years at Urbana he remained under the influences of this cult; but in his Cornell years he seems to have been regarded as decidedly liberal in his religious convictions.[73] In 1886 he and his family became members of Saint George's Episcopal Church. His membership was later transferred to Saint Bartholomew's Church; he remained a member of this parish until his death.[74]

[72] Information provided by Austa Boyesen.
[73] *Open Court,* 10:4812–4813.
[74] Information provided by Austa Boyesen.

On June 27, 1878, when he was still at Ithaca, Boyesen married Elizabeth Morris Keen, the daughter of a business man in the city of Chicago. The dedication verses in the *Idylls of Norway*, " to L. K. B.," are evidently addressed to her.

> I fain would praise thee with surpassing praise
> To whom my soul its first allegiance gave,
> For thou art fair as thou art wise and brave.
> And, like the lily that with sweet amaze
> Rocks on its lake and spreads it golden rays
> Serenely to the sun and knows not why,
> Thou spreadst the tranquil splendor of thine eyes
> Upon my heart and fillst the happy days
> Brimmed with the fragrance and the light of thee.

In the same volume he published a group of ten sonnets, " To Lillie," some of which show a tenderness and a depth of feeling that are not always found in his verse.[75]

Three sons were born in the Boyesen household: Hjalmar Hjorth, Algernon, and Bayard.[76] The father dedicated a volume of a dozen short stories to his " three little lovely vikings," [77] the oldest of whom had seen about eight years at the time. The dedicatory verses in this volume are perhaps the most delightful that the poet-author ever penned. One may surmise that they were suggested by Longfellow's " The Children's Hour"; but Boyesen's treatment is wholly original and owes nothing to the art of the bard of Cambridge.

Hjalmar was the first to arrive.

> With a lusty Norseland war whoop
> He came in the dead of night.

He had queer ways and subjected his family to a highly effective form of despotism:

[75] In the family Mrs. Boyesen was always called " Lillie."

[76] Hjalmar Hjorth Boyesen II was born in Ithaca, July 7, 1879. After some years in the field of magazine journalism, he turned his attention to the law. He died August 29, 1929. Algernon Boyesen was born on October 13, 1881. He followed the professions of journalism and literature. He died in 1930. Bayard Boyesen was born in 1883 (?). For a term of years he was a member of the faculty of Columbia University, teaching principally English.

[77] *The Modern Vikings* (New York, 1887).

He sang in the small hours of morning
And dined in the middle of night.

After the household had been thoroughly subdued,

He summoned his brother Alger
From the realm beyond the foam.

. . . .
And he is a laughing tyrant
With dimples and golden curls.

Last of all came Bayard

As chivalrous as your name!

. . . .
Vain and stubborn and tender
Fair son of the valiant North
With a voice like the storm and the north wind
When it sweeps from the glaciers forth.

Boyesen was an enthusiastic American. He took his naturalization seriously and reserved no allegiance in any form to his native land. At the same time he had a large measure of racial pride. He attributed his physical vigor and his robust health to a strong ancestry and to the hardening influences of northern life. Like his sons he was a viking and liked to speak of himself as of viking stock.

A few years before his death he was seized with a yearning to see his native land once more. He had last visited Norway in 1873, eighteen or nineteen years before. His visit, in 1891, proved an almost bitter disappointment. The land was much as before, interesting, lovely, enchanting, but the people had changed. Reluctantly he had to accept the distressing fact that he was no longer a Norwegian.[78]

"It was the feeling that I had in a measure forfeited the right to apply it [*the term 'native'*] to myself which caused me a vague heartache during my recent visit to Norway." A residence of twenty-two years in another land had made decided changes in his spiritual being, greater than he could have imagined. To his surprise he had discovered that his earlier skill in using the Norwegian language had

[78] *Columbia University Bulletin*, no. 12, p. 49.

in part been lost. At least his speech was not so fluent and dependable as he had believed it was and would be. After his return he rarely spoke Norwegian and he never visited his native land again.[79]

In the autumn of 1895 he had just completed his forty-seventh year. He was in the best years of middle age and his friends predicted that a man with such an apparently robust constitution would surely have a long life. Boyesen had, however, certain premonitions of coming ills. In a recent letter to a friend he had complained that his usual elasticity was no longer so dependable as earlier. Weariness was stealing upon him, and that was not a good sign.[80]

When the new year began at the university, he was at hand and at work in the usual way. He had found temporary quarters where he expected to remain till his family should return from their summer home at Southampton, Long Island, a month or two later. On Wednesday, October 2, he seemed well as usual, but during the night he was taken with a severe chill. A physician was called in the morning and his examination led him to suspect pneumonia. About noon the next day Boyesen passed away. The swift progress of the disease was doubtless promoted by a heart ailment with which the patient had apparently been afflicted for some time but which had not been regarded as serious.[81]

On the following Tuesday, October 8, Boyesen was buried from Saint Bartholomew's Church, the Reverend Robert C. Booth officiating. The faculty and students of Columbia College attended in a body. Colleagues and friends of the literary profession bore him to the grave. The body was taken to Kensico burial ground and there laid to rest.[82]

[79] Boyesen, *Literary and Social Silhouettes,* 194 (New York, 1894); *Columbia University Bulletin,* no. 12, p. 49.
[80] *Columbia University Bulletin,* no. 12, p. 46.
[81] *Nordstjernan* (New York), October 10, 1895.
[82] The list of pallbearers is significant of the high place that Boyesen had won for himself in the academic and literary professions. Among them were some of his most prominent colleagues in Columbia University: President Seth Low and Professors J. H. van Amringe, Nicholas Murray Butler, Munroe Smith, Brander Matthews, and W. H. Carpenter. The list further includes such well

A final honor was paid to the Boyesen family by the university trustees shortly after the funeral. At Columbia the sons and daughters of the members of the faculty were (and presumably still are) permitted to register as students without the payment of tuition. Normally this privilege expires on the death of the father; but in the case of the Boyesen family it was allowed to continue till Bayard, the youngest of the three sons, had completed his university work.[88]

known names as William Dean Howells, E. C. Stedman, Richard Watson Gilder, Hamilton W. Mabie, Carl Schurz, Charles S. Fairchild, Salem H. Wales, John DeWitt Warner, J. Brisben Walker, and Dr. Gaillard Thomas; *Critic*, 27: 237; *Columbia University Bulletin*, no. 12, p. 45.

[88] There seems to be no authority for the statement in Lamb's *Biographical Dictionary of the United States*, 1:370, that Boyesen's sons were made the wards of Columbia University. Evidently the author of the sketch misunderstood the action of the trustees.

In the late autumn of 1850 a quarter of a century had passed since the first Norwegian settlement had been formed on American soil. A survey of conditions as they were in that year would have revealed a growing number of Norse communities, located chiefly in southern Wisconsin and northern Illinois. Some of these could boast a considerable number of families and farms, but most of them were feeble and small, having enjoyed a brief existence only.

Such a survey would also have revealed that in many of these localities there was very little in the way of organized institutional life except such as was fostered by the local government. In most cases this was limited to the public school. One would be struck especially by the fact that the church, which was to become such a vital influence in the life of the rural settlements, had as yet attained only a very imperfect organization.

When the year 1850 began, the clerical forces that served the Lutheran churches in these settlements numbered only five regularly ordained men. Of these only one, Hans Andreas Stub, the revered pastor in old Muskego, could claim the distinction of a university degree. His four colleagues belonged in a wholly different category; they were gifted laymen without any formal theological training who had been set apart for the service and duties of the pulpit and the altar. It was only natural that such ministers should continue to regard the problems of the church from the layman's point of view.

Later in the year Adolph C. Preus arrived in Wisconsin to take charge of an extensive and important parish in the Koshkonong area. Three men came in 1851: Hans Amberg Preus, N. O. Brandt, and G. F. Dietrichson. The following year the group received a notable addition in Jacob Aal Ottesen, who after some years in Manitowoc succeeded A. C. Preus in the Koshkonong churches.

These men, with C. L. Clausen (who was a Dane and whose background differed markedly from that of his Norse brethren), organized the Norwegian Synod in 1853. They were all able men and devoted pastors and among them were two who had the will, the energy, and the peculiar abilities that make for leadership: H. A. Preus and J. A. Ottesen. In the years ahead these two were to carry the heaviest burdens in constructive undertakings. They were also to lead in religious controversy, of which there was much in preparation. Both were young men; in 1853 they were twenty-eight years old.

The new church body received a powerful reinforcement in the same year, when Ulrik Vilhelm Koren arrived to take a pastorate in northeastern Iowa. Of men who came later particular mention must be made of Laurentius Larsen and Bernt Julius Muus, who emigrated respectively in 1857 and 1859.

These five men, Preus, Ottesen, Koren, Larsen, and Muus, were the architects of the Norwegian Synod. For more than a generation they were the trusted guides. They had many things in common. Their families belonged to the educated, one may say to the aristocratic, class. With one possible exception they had ancestors of Danish or German origin, as such names as Preus, Koren, and Muus abundantly testify. Most of them had grown up in the homes of civil officials, clergymen, school administrators, or officers in the army. All had degrees from the national university. In their theological studies all had been guided, if not by the same teachers, at least by teachers who were of the same general theological tendency. In the New World they became close personal friends and found much enjoyment in their reciprocal social relations.

It was therefore to be expected that these men and their

immigrant colleagues should see eye to eye on most subjects, and for a long time the group displayed a remarkable solidarity. As problem after problem arose in the church these leaders faced what opposition there was in undisturbed unity. Their wise strategy, their clear-cut argumentation, and their diplomatic skill usually carried the day.

There was much in the institutional system of the great republic that these men regarded with enthusiastic approval. They believed in western democracy and strove to live according to its precepts. At the same time they found customs and arrangements which they could not accept with any degree of cordiality. One of these was the common school.

Even as early as the year of its organization the leaders of the Synod had looked askance at the common school.[1] The objections raised by the ministerial critics were many, but three were fundamental: the common school was irreligious; it was inefficient; it was not suited to the needs of the Norwegian pioneers.

The pastorate of the new church body stressed heavily the importance of a positively Christian education. By this the leaders meant not only instruction in religious subjects, but, more fundamentally, a system of instruction that should be instinct with a religious spirit. While placing due emphasis on the need of conversion, they seemed to believe that a mind properly instructed in Christian fundamentals would be more likely to heed the divine commands than one that had not received the light that is derived from Christian teaching. And such enlightenment could not be expected from a school from which religion was carefully excluded.

There were other reasons, too, why these clergymen found it difficult to accept this characteristically American insti-

[1] *Skandinaven,* May 26, 1869. The public school system in Wisconsin dates from 1848. There were free public schools in Illinois in the earlier years of statehood but they were not numerous till about 1850 when the system finally was placed on a solid foundation.

tution. Having been educated in the Old World, they knew the Norwegian school system in all its grades and they were naturally impressed by its many excellences. Several of them had been employed as teachers before emigration; those who have been enumerated among the leaders had all served in this capacity. It is therefore easy to understand why they had assumed an attitude of opposition. Their ideal was a system of education inspired by Lutheran principles, one that would teach effectively the essentials of the Lutheran religion, using such books and methods as they were acquainted with and employing in considerable part the Norwegian language as a vehicle of instruction.

The charge of inefficiency was one that the friends of the common school could not readily refute. In pioneer communities the schools were too often anything but effective. The Norwegians complained that the school authorities employed too many young girls, most of whom were uninformed as well as immature. Coming from a country where a teacher might enjoy almost a life tenure, they could not understand the American practice of frequent change. Time came when they were to change their minds on much of this, especially on the expediency of employing women in the schoolroom;[2] but in the 1850's and even later the good men of the conservative tendency firmly believed that woman's place was not in the schoolhouse.

The third objection, that the "Yankee school" could not meet the needs of immigrant communities, was endorsed by many who were not vitally interested in promoting religious education. Norwegian families, these men held, were best served by Norwegian schools. This nationalistic feeling is something that the historian cannot afford to ignore. In those days of the sixties and for at least two decades longer it was believed in many quarters to be supremely necessary to maintain Norwegian wherever possible as a

[2] See Karen Larsen, *Laur. Larsen, Pioneer College President,* 330-331 (Northfield, Minnesota, 1936).

living language on American soil. Some of the leaders in
this opinion believed that while it was, of course, necessary
for their children to learn English, that language need not be
studied before the pupils had completed their twelfth or
thirteenth year. In other words the social and intellectual
life of a child should be of the Norwegian pattern till the
year of confirmation. By that time the mother tongue
would have become " the language of the child's heart,"
and as such would hold a preferred place till the end of life.

The conservative wing of the clergy had set itself a problem. How could it best be solved?

II

In the decade of the 1860's it was becoming evident that
the spiritual needs of the Norwegian settlements could not
be supplied, as had been hoped, by the mother church in
Norway. By the close of 1865 about seventy-eight thousand
Norsemen had emigrated to the New World.[3] Two years
later H. A. Preus reported that only twenty Norwegian
theologians had come to accept parishes in the Northwest
and of these three had returned to Norway.[4] It seemed
necessary therefore to devise ways and means to prepare
men for the ministry in this country. But to build, equip,
and man a seminary was beyond the powers of the pioneer
church. Apparently the only practical solution of the problem was to find some Lutheran institution already established which might be willing to receive Norwegian students
and to train them for pastoral work.

In the spring of 1857 N. O. Brandt and J. A. Ottesen,
with credentials from the Norwegian Synod, set forth to spy
out the land. They visited seminaries in Columbus, Buf-
falo, and St. Louis, but only in St. Louis did they seem to
find what the church needed. What the great Walther and

[3] Theodore C. Blegen, *Norwegian Migration to America*, 349–350 (Northfield,
Minnesota, 1931).
[4] *Syv foredrag om de kirkelige forhold blandt de norske i Amerika*, 43
(Christiania, 1867).

the Missouri Synod had achieved at Concordia Seminary impressed them mightily.[5] The outcome was that arrangements were made for the education of young Norsemen in the theological institutions of the Missouri Synod, an arrangement that stood for approximately two decades.

The theologians at St. Louis contributed heavily to the development of the Norwegian church. They gave precision and clarity to its dogmatic system. They impressed upon the clergy their ideals of the life and government of a free church. The relationship no doubt also had its less favorable side; one weakness was the emphasis on German to the almost complete exclusion of English. At any rate, some of the men who returned from Concordia to take up pastoral work among their own people were not profoundly impressed with the need of a thorough mastery of English and did little to promote its use in the Norwegian settlements.

Among other things that they brought home from St Louis was what seemed to be a practical solution of the problem of primary education. The Germans had found it possible to build up an extensive system of parochial schools; why should the Norwegians hesitate longer to adopt a similar policy? The more the leaders of the Synod reflected on the virtues of parochial education, the more thoroughly convinced they became that the " Yankee school" was a very flimsy arrangement.

In 1859 the annual meeting of the Synod was held in Coon Valley in southwestern Wisconsin. The question of Christian education was on the agenda and two conclusions were reached:

1. It was agreed that members of the church might properly employ tutors (*huslærere*), but the work of such teachers should be under the supervision of the congregation.

2. The meeting was unwilling to approve a proposal to exclude from the church all who should refuse to support

[5] See the report of the delegates in J. A. Bergh, *Den norsk lutherske kirkes historie i Amerika*, 138–144 (Minneapolis, 1914).

schools of religion. It was believed that the local situation would have to dictate what action should be taken in such cases.[6]

Two years later the nation was at war fighting for its very life. Like so many other controversial issues the school question was allowed to lie dormant till the mighty conflict had come to its end. But after the war the discussion was resumed; and for more than a decade it raged across the entire Northwest.

The debate began in earnest after the synodical convention in Manitowoc in 1866.[7] At this meeting the Synod adopted a definite educational policy based on a series of twenty-seven propositions which covered almost every aspect of the problem. This platform was the work of a committee, some of the members of which were intimately acquainted with the system that had been developed in the Missouri Synod. Consequently there was real basis for the charge (which was promptly raised) that the parochial school idea was a borrowing from Missouri. Since the entire ministerium was favorably disposed toward the policies of the great German synod, it was not difficult to get the report of the committee adopted. Some of its more important propositions read as follows:

2. In this country it must, therefore, as a rule be regarded as desirable for Christians to establish such parochial schools as can give instruction in subjects comparable to those taught in the so-called " common schools " so that these need not be patronized.

3. It is our duty as citizens to support these common schools even if we do not entrust our children to them.

4. These non-religious public schools give their best service to those elements in our population which are not Christian and do not crave a Christian education.

5. The fact that religion is not taught in these schools is a necessary result of the religious freedom which it is our good fortune to enjoy under our national system of government; but it is also a melancholy testimony to the apostasy of our time and to the division of the church due to the activity of the sects.

[6] *Emigranten* (Madison, Wisconsin), October 22, 1859. The convention was in session October 14–18.

[7] Editorial review of the controversy in *Skandinaven*, April 21, 1869. See also the issue of May 26, 1869.

15. It must be possible for us to establish parochial schools of such a character that we shall not need to patronize the American common schools, as other Christians have done, including groups who speak foreign languages.

18. Where such an arrangement as the one recommended above cannot be made or cannot be achieved at an early date, the members of our congregations must seek to acquire as great an influence as possible in the management of the district schools, particularly in the appointment of teachers and in determining the time of its sessions.

20. Wherever no other arrangement seems practicable, it must be regarded as sufficient for the preparation in English to send the children to the public schools after confirmation, though not earlier.[8]

In this platform the issues were clearly indicated. They were further defined by H. A. Preus in a lecture delivered in Oslo the following year: "It is our purpose and endeavor to organize our church schools in such a way as to render the English public schools superfluous, so far as our church members are concerned."[9] This, he admitted, could only mean that the subjects taught in the common school would have to be introduced into the plan of parochial school instruction. There would no doubt be difficulties about taxation; still, "we must labor to attain this end." The public schools, he allowed, were not necessarily evil. The trouble was that they did not give adequate instruction. They were weak because of a continuous change of teachers. They were useless to the Norwegian pioneer because they were not Lutheran.[10]

III

On May 2, 1866, there appeared in Chicago the first issue of a new Dano-Norwegian weekly bearing the name *Skandinaven*. The publishers were John Anderson, a young printer, and Knud Langeland, an older man who had once been associated with a venture in Free-Soil journalism. Langeland, as the more experienced of the two, took the

[8] Preus, *Syv foredrag*, 32 ff. See p 306 of Hamre
[9] Preus, *Syv foredrag*, 32.
[10] Preus, *Syv foredrag*, 32 ff.

editorial chair, and under his capable management the new journal soon attained to a position of real influence among the Norsemen in the Northwest.

Langeland's views were definite and precise and he knew how to express them in clear and forceful Norwegian. Both he and his associate had leanings toward the left wing element in the Lutheran church; but positive propaganda in this direction was not a part of the editorial policy. Almost at the very beginning of its career *Skandinaven* came into conflict with the Norwegian Synod. The editor would not admit, however, that his paper harbored any general hostile feeling toward this great church body. His opposition was limited to certain "Missourian" views on slavery and the common school; on these questions he refused to be silent, and the war was on.[11]

The editor was able to show many reasons why his paper should come out in opposition to the Manitowoc platform. There was, to begin with, the economic consideration. The proposed system would, he believed, add an insupportable burden to the heavy load of debt that had already been assumed by the Norwegian farmers, who in most cases had come from the steerage with empty hands. He could also point to a real dearth of qualified teachers, especially of such as were able to give adequate instruction in English. In mixed communities the two schools, the public and the parochial, would of necessity have to exist side by side, with nothing remarkable in either case except poverty and weakness. Langeland was thoroughly convinced that parochial schools would be for a long time of low efficiency; and ineffective teaching could not give to the young Norwegians what the changing times required.

But Langeland did not rest his case at this point; he was not satisfied with a merely negative position. His favorite argument was that a full-blown system of church schools

[11] *Skandinaven*, June 30, 1874. The statement is by Langeland's successor, Professor Svein Nilsson.

was wholly unnecessary; that the belief in their necessity was an importation from St. Louis, from the theologians of which city the conservative clergy had received other ideas, too, which the Norwegian laity had refused to accept; and, finally, that the public school was a highly meritorious institution which, moreover, as American citizens, his countrymen were in duty bound to patronize and support.[12]

Langeland's critics usually sent their communications to *Fædrelandet og emigranten*, a newspaper published in La Crosse, Wisconsin.[13] While this paper was by no means an organ of the Norwegian Synod, the editor accepted the viewpoint of Muus and Preus and consequently was favorable to parochial schools. Occasionally he came into direct conflict with his colleague in Chicago but that was a rare occurrence. Ordinarily he left the field of controversy to his contributors, whom he knew to be resourceful both in attack and defense.

For more than a decade the debate continued. Keen weapons were used on both sides. Langeland expressed a desire to believe that H. A. Preus and C. M. Hvistendahl were honest in their opposition to the common school; evidently his faith was not strong. He wrote with feeling about "the German-Missouri strait jacket, tyranny, and hierarchical domineering";[14] he even went so far as to question whether opposition to the public school might not be regarded as treason.[15]

Naturally the clergy resented bitterly these innuendos. One may be sure that they were neither dishonest nor disloyal, though one is safe in affirming that they were not always discreet. Meanwhile the sense of wrong prompted them to reply in kind; H. A. Preus spoke of his opponents

---

[12] *Skandinaven*, May 26, 1869, and *passim*.

[13] *Fædrelandet* (published in La Crosse) and *Emigranten* (published in Madison) were consolidated in 1868 and appeared in combined form on September 3 of that year.

[14] *Skandinaven*, May 26, 1869. C. M. Hvistendahl was at the time in charge of the old parish at Muskego. He was an uncompromising enemy of the common school.

[15] *Fædrelandet og emigranten*, October 15, 1868.

as "malicious defamers." *Skandinaven,* in Muus's opinion, was a "wicked, ungodly newspaper." And there were those who affirmed in all seriousness that Langeland and his associates "labored to promote the kingdom of Satan."[16]

IV

In October, 1865, the friends of Luther College were gathering in Decorah to celebrate a notable achievement: a college building had been completed and was now to be dedicated. It was to be a joyous occasion and such it no doubt turned out to be. Still, the joy was not unmixed, for when the celebrants reached the campus they learned that the students had called a strike.

There was much dissatisfaction among the young men and no doubt some of it was justified. Discipline was severe and duties were manifold and onerous; at least so the students thought. The uprising was led by Rasmus B. Anderson, who later achieved fame in many fields; but at the time he was merely a young student with large ambitions, a restless disposition, and no lack of confidence in his own self. The rebellion eventuated in Anderson's expulsion. His sins were later forgiven but he was denied readmission.[17] Ultimately he received a degree from the college, but that was after twenty-five years.

The young rebel was not daunted. A few weeks after the affair in Decorah he proceeded, with the help of Erik Ellefsen, a prominent Norseman in the neighboring Big Canoe settlement, to organize an "education society," which actually achieved a membership of about one hundred. The professed purpose of the society was to found a college, to be located, perhaps, in Minnesota. This institution was to be built, not like the college in Decorah, on the principles of the Norwegian Latin school, but on those of the older American institutions. It was to be headed — such was actually

[16] *Skandinaven,* April 7 and May 26, 1869; December 15, 1874.
[17] See Anderson's own account of the uprising in *Life Story of Rasmus B. Anderson,* 47–57 (Madison, Wisconsin, 1915).

the plan — by Rasmus Anderson, who had now attained the advanced age of nineteen years. Since none of the members knew what an American college was like, it would be necessary, first of all, to send the future president to some eastern institution, possibly to Yale, to complete his education.[18]

Less than a year later Anderson was able to convince the authorities of Albion Academy that it would be expedient to add a Norwegian teacher to the Albion faculty and that he was the proper man for that position. This change in his fortunes led to a corresponding change in the program of the education society. From now on it was to work for the appointment of Norwegian teachers at American institutions, first of all at the University of Wisconsin and Beloit College.[19]

In the summer of 1868 the Synod met in annual convention in Chicago. When time came for the East Koshkonong Church to select a delegate to this meeting, someone suggested Anderson. The pastor, Ottesen, tried to prevent his election, fearing that to give credentials to the erstwhile student might not be wise. He was not successful. Anderson went to Chicago.

Anderson's presence at the convention was highly embarrassing to the leaders, and when he arose to move a series of amendments to the Manitowoc platform, there was a disposition to refuse him the right to the floor. But B. J. Muus, though not kindly disposed toward Anderson, believed above all in the freedom of speech and the young delegate was allowed to present his program. Anderson urged the church to accept the common school, but to work for the appointment of Norwegian Lutheran teachers in Norwegian communities. These teachers might be employed to conduct Norwegian or church school when the public school was not in session. He also proposed that the Norwegian language should be taught in the common school wherever there was a real demand for it. Finally he urged

[18] Anderson, *Life Story*, 71–72.
[19] Anderson, *Life Story*, 75–79.

that an effort be made to have Norwegian teachers appointed in the higher American schools.[20]

Anderson's proposals were received in silence; they were not discussed. He did not long remain idle. His plan now was to revive his education society and to work for its extension throughout the Northwest. He got into communication with some of the leaders in Norsedom, men like C. L. Clausen, John A. Johnson, and Knud Langeland. The outcome was that Clausen called a meeting to organize a Lutheran education society, setting the date at March 4, 1869.[21]

The meeting was held in the courthouse in Madison on the specified day. About three hundred had responded to the call. Never before had such a representative body of Norsemen gathered to discuss the subject of education. In the movement were men like Halle Steensland, Svein Nilsson, C. F. Solberg, and Just Caen. Many appeared to be enthusiastic for an organization like the one proposed; but there were also those who came to the meeting with hostile intent. Among the more outspoken critics H. A. Preus and C. M. Hvistendahl were the leaders. On the other hand O. J. Hatlestad, S. M. Krogness, and M. Falk Gjertsen, who were all of the left wing of the church and held membership in the Scandinavian Augustana Synod, were disposed to follow the lead of Anderson and Clausen.[22]

There were doubts in many minds as to the real objective of the gathering. Some hoped that it was to make plans for a university. But the outcome of the discussion was that the new society could achieve most by working for the establishment of Norwegian professorships in American colleges.[23] It was hoped that by this arrangement young Norwegians would be able to qualify for teaching positions in the public schools. In the newspaper debate that followed the

[20] Anderson, Life Story, 98–99; Skandinaven, July 22, 1868.
[21] Anderson, Life Story, 117.
[22] For an account of the meeting see Fædrelandet og emigranten, March 11, 1869. Solberg, Nilsson, and Caen were of the journalistic profession. Caen's presence (he was a Jew) was not relished by all the participants.
[23] Skandinaven, April 21 and May 12, 1869.

adjournment of the meeting, it came out, however, that the ultimate object was after all the founding of a university. After the projected professorships had been established and manned, they might, it was hoped, be withdrawn and brought together into a university faculty.[24]

The following day a group of about forty dissenters met and passed resolutions condemning the professorship plan. Later in the spring this element met in West Koshkonong Church to discuss a constructive program. Ottesen urged the establishment of a series of "middle schools" or what we should probably call high schools. Enthusiasm was, however, at a low ebb. Attention was called to the indebtedness that still hung over Luther College. Few believed that the settlements were strong enough to realize Ottesen's plan.[25]

On the day when the Madison meeting convened, the La Crosse journal published a letter from the veteran pastor, A. C. Preus, in which the plans attributed to Anderson and Clausen were examined and in part condemned. Preus gave a qualified approval to the common school; he would seek to improve it and, wherever possible, he would have it conducted by Lutheran teachers. But for higher education in America he had nothing good to say; the colleges were infidel in their teaching and blasphemous in their mode of instruction (*gudsfornægtende og gudsbespottende*). With such schools no right-believing Lutheran could have anything to do. The Synod now had its college, and wherever possible there should be parochial schools. In between he would establish middle schools.[26] Such was the plan that was now taking form in conservative circles.

Preus's letter called forth several vigorous replies, the strongest of which was a somewhat irate editorial in *Skandinaven*. In this Langeland bemoaned the fact that a Nor-

[24] *Skandinaven,* April 14 and 28, 1869: letters by C. M. Hvistendahl and S. M. Krognæs.
[25] *Fædrelandet og emigranten,* May 6, 1869; *Skandinaven,* May 12, 1869.
[26] *Fædrelandet og emigranten,* March 4, 1869.

wegian clergyman could go so far as publicly to attack, in the coarsest and most dishonoring manner, one of the primary institutions of the land to which he was so deeply indebted. In reply to Preus's condemnation of higher American education Langeland stated his belief that there could be no real conflict between religious truth and scientific knowledge.[27]

Preus was ably seconded by Hvistendahl, who could not support the professorship plan but believed in the feasibility of establishing independent schools. Among the defenders of the movement was S. M. Krogness, who had served for some years as teacher in the schools of Norway. Man, said Krogness, has a double citizenship, secular and spiritual, each of which has its rightful claim. He did not fear the American school system (he sent his own children to the common school), if the studies there could be supplemented with formal instruction in religion. He would like a division of time between secular and religious instruction but feared that economic considerations would prevent the successful adoption of any plan of this sort.[28]

At the Madison meeting a Lutheran Education Society had been organized with the usual staff of officials, including trustees and an executive committee. Its history proved to be short. A second meeting was held early in June, 1870, in Decorah. At this meeting the society reaffirmed its stand on the subject of Scandinavian professorships in the higher schools. In addition the discussion revealed a strong opinion that teachers must be trained for the teaching of Norwegian as well as English in the common schools.[29] This opinion took account of a new situation in Wisconsin, where, the year before, the legislature had passed a bill sponsored by Assemblyman Knute Nelson, which permitted the teaching

[27] *Skandinaven*, April 7 and 14, 1869.
[28] *Skandinaven*, May 12 and 26, 1869.
[29] *Fremad*, June 16, 1870. At this meeting John A. Johnson was chosen to succeed C. L. Clausen as president. Hans Borchsenius, a Dane, was elected secretary. See also the issue of May 19, 1870.

of foreign languages in the public schools of the state.[30] Thus, by inference at least, the society placed its stamp of approval on the common school.

After 1870 nothing more was heard of the education society. It was a symptom of revolt against certain tendencies in the Norwegian church, but it was premature and could not succeed. It was not without results, however, for it served to give the current discussion a wider field. After 1870, though the common school remained the chief subject of contention, the controversy had come to include the entire system of American education.

V

During the decade of the seventies the leadership in the fight for Norwegian parochial schools was held by Bernt Julius Muus, a vigorous pastor who served a large group of settlements in Goodhue County, Minnesota, and adjacent parts. Muus was a man with a somewhat peculiar but arresting personality. He was a clear thinker. His conclusions were definite, if not always well founded. His views were often extreme and he stated them without any view to conciliation or accommodation. Early in 1870, when the question of the common school was again coming into prominence, it was he who struck the keynote on the conservative side, "I regard the common school as an institution which because of its essential principle (efter sit princip) must work in opposition to the kingdom of God; furthermore, I regard it as a feeble device, inasmuch as the children in those schools learn much less than they can and ought."[31]

In developing the last thought Muus wrote that the pupils may "perhaps read some romance or other entitled the history of the United States." Even if it was not always sinful

[30] Statement by Knute Nelson in *Skandinaven*, April 14, 1869. A bill introduced by Nelson in 1868 had failed to pass. Encouraged by A. C. Preus to reintroduce it, he did so in the following session and secured favorable action.
[31] *Fædrelandet og emigranten*, March 10, 1870.

to send children to the public schools, it was, at least, a waste of good money. He further stated his conviction that the American public had grown weary of its educational system and would gladly see it abolished, since it was clearly a hindrance to true education.[32]

Muus's deliverance on " Schools and a Good School " was interpreted as a call to arms by both sides. John A. Johnson, who was in those days the most prominent Norwegian layman in the country, penned an early reply. It was the duty of parents, he argued, to give their children such an education as would make them effective citizens. The smaller communities could not, in his opinion, provide adequate schools out of their own means. Moreover, the common school was not an evil thing as Muus contended. It had many virtues and deserved support.[33]

A little later Halle Steensland, also of Madison and an influential member of the Synod, came out in defense of the public school. He could not discover the dangers that Muus appeared to see. To abandon the American system would be to go back to the Middle Ages.[34]

A. J. Berdahl of Fillmore County, Minnesota, varied the discussion with an attack on parochial schools. He insisted that children educated in the common schools were no more wicked than those who were instructed in parochial schools. Nor did he find anything immoral in the American textbooks. On the other hand the Norwegian schoolbooks were not good and Norwegian parochial schools would get nowhere until better books could be provided.[35] To this the editor who published Berdahl's letter remarked that while the English textbooks might not be exactly immoral, they were the product not of Lutheran but of Reformed authors and therefore remained objectionable.

[32] *Fædrelandet og emigranten,* March 10, 1870.
[33] *Skandinaven,* April 13, 1870; *Fædrelandet og emigranten,* April 21 and May 4, 1870.
[34] *Fædrelandet og emigranten,* June 23, 1870.
[35] *Fædrelandet og emigranten,* August 3, 1871.

Another layman writing from Minnesota asked the editor of *Skandinaven* whether he believed that children could get the necessary Christian education in the public schools. This gave Langeland an opportunity to restate his position. His answer was " No." Religious instruction, he held, was essential to education but it could be and would have to be provided by other agencies: the home, the Sunday school, or the school of religion. At a later date the editor affirmed that it was the purpose of his paper "to oppose and to obstruct any system of education, the aim of which is to keep our people in an alien state or condition beyond the limits of necessity."[36]

Early in 1872 Langeland resigned his editorial duties and was succeeded by Svein Nilsson, an elderly journalist who was already in the service as associate editor.[37] Nilsson was in entire sympathy with the educational views of his militant predecessor and could be trusted to continue his editorial policy. In his first leading article he advised the Synod to accept the public school as other Protestant churches had done. He argued that if Norwegians were to take the place in American life to which their citizenship entitled them, an adequate education would be the first requisite. Moreover, he contended, and this was a new argument, the church should not aim at any control of education except in the matter of religion.[38]

In a later editorial Svein Nilsson deplored the practice of criticizing the public schools, since violent talk of this sort encouraged parents to neglect them. Nor could he agree with some of his friends that teachers should be appointed for indefinite terms. If the patrons of a school deemed it expedient to hire a new teacher they had the right to do so.

[36] *Skandinaven*, February 22 and May 17, 1871.
[37] Langeland published his valedictory in the issue of May 22, 1872. The career of his successor, Svein Nilsson, is sketched by D. G. Ristad in Norwegian-American Historical Association, *Studies and Records*, 9:29–37 (Northfield, Minnesota, 1936).
[38] *Skandinaven*, May 29, 1872.

Of the wisdom of such a change they alone would be in position to judge.[39]

The Synod resumed discussion of primary education at its annual meeting in July, 1873. The debate centered about an elaborate statement of the problem, prepared and presented by H. A. Preus. Again the church was asked to pledge itself to support the common school, it being "necessary because of the prevailing indifference to religion." Of course, the ideal remained the parochial school. Only when the public schools were conducted by Lutheran teachers who maintained Christian discipline could they be recommended to members of the church.[40]

The following year the convention met in Holden Church in one of the many parishes served by the redoubtable B. J. Muus. *Skandinaven* was represented in the person of John A. Johnson, who had come to report the proceedings. When Muus heard of his presence he protested; "a paper so hostile to the Christian religion (*ukristeligt*) as *Skandinaven*" should not be allowed to have a reporter at the meeting. The protest was overruled, however, and Johnson remained.[41]

In the discussion of educational policy Muus led with a series of theses embodying his own well known personal views. Since the eternal welfare of the children is more important than their secular welfare, and since there is salvation in God's Word only, that subject, he held, must be made a part of the child's education. The evil thing about the common school is that it entices the child away from the Saviour. His position is summed up in the following interesting statement:

Since one may be justified on occasions of dire necessity in subjecting oneself and others to great temptations, one must not insist that it would be sinful under all circumstances to patronize the common school; nevertheless, it is the duty of all Christians

[39] *Skandinaven,* April 8 and May 6, 1873.
[40] *Skandinaven,* July 22 and 29, 1873.
[41] *Budstikken,* June 23, 1874; John A. Johnson in *Skandinaven,* December 15, 1874.

according to their strength and abilities to strive to provide Christian schools for their children.[42]

It was inevitable that the ancient problem of the relationship of church to state should come up in the discussion of these questions. Muus and II. A. Preus insisted that the duty of the state was to help the parents. If these two forces should come into collision, the state must yield to the church. Parents might find it their duty, even in secular matters, to refuse obedience. This principle did not, however, find general acceptance. V. Koren, A. Mikkelsen, and F. A. Schmidt believed that parents must obey the laws unless they are contrary to the Word of God. Parents, they held, were not allowed to choose what laws they would obey. If the laws were hostile to conscience, the only escape might be emigration.[43]

The Muus proposals were neither accepted nor rejected. Evidently there were those who felt that the pastor's theory was too rigid. Laur. Larsen, while still in favor of parochial schools, could discover no hidden peril in the subjects taught in the common school, and there were some who raised the question whether it was not inimical to the welfare of the children to refuse them state education.[44]

Meanwhile the icy hand of the great depression that came with the panic of 1873 lay with its deadening weight across the entire land. Men's thoughts were more and more concerned with the economics of life. A parochial school system might be desirable, but could the church afford it?

VI

The controversy raged on with unabated vigor till the close of the seventies. As the years passed by, new forces appeared on the field of decision; most of these were marshaled on the side of *Skandinaven* and the common school.

[42] *Skandinaven,* July 21, 1874.
[43] *Budstikken,* July 4, 1874.
[44] *Budstikken,* July 4, 1874; *Skandinaven,* July 21, 1874.

Among these newer participants were two weekly newspapers, *Budstikken,* which first saw the light in Minneapolis in 1872, and *Norden,* the first number of which came from a press in Chicago on October 13, 1874.

Budstikken was somewhat anticlerical from the first issue and was naturally regarded by the conservatives as a foe to religion. This indictment the editors, of course, denied; for though the paper urged its readers to support and patronize the common schools as a matter of civic duty, it also favored a system of schools of religion as supplementary institutions. Parochial schools might properly be established where the public schools were inadequate.[45] This concession was of slight value, however, since, as conditions were at the time, it was scarcely possible for the church schools to attain a degree of efficiency comparable to that of the public schools.

Norden was a conservative publication and the conservative leaders of the clergy hoped much from it. In these hopes they were disappointed. The editor, Halvard Hande, was indeed a clergyman and a member of the Norwegian Synod; but he seems to have disliked controversy and he saw clearly the danger in assuming extreme positions. Moreover, the problem of education, as viewed from an editorial chair in Chicago, proved to have angles and facets that were not clearly visible to pastors in the rural settlements.

For two or three years Hande had little to say about the common school. He seemed to be doing nothing directly to mold or to direct opinion. Nevertheless, it was evident that his leanings were toward the school system approved by Muus and Preus and Hvistendahl. A disagreement with *Skandinaven* was, of course, inevitable, for the "Old Lady in Chicago" was quite sensitive to heresy in the matter of the public school. Svein Nilsson, while admitting that Hande was more liberal than his clerical brethren, was sure that he could see in *Norden* an indirect opponent of American education.[46]

[45] June 5, 1875; June 10, 1879.
[46] *Skandinaven,* February 26, 1878.

Hande was willing to admit a partiality for parochial schools, if the instruction could be given in English. Svein Nilsson at once came back with the old questions: Where are the teachers? [47] Where are the men who are adequately prepared to teach both languages? To these questions no one had as yet been able to find a satisfactory reply. There were indeed teachers among the immigrants, but many of them found their way into the ministerial profession and very few became thoroughly conversant with the English language.

It may seem strange that down to the middle of the seventies the churches of the left wing had taken only a small part in the controversy. Among the ministers of the Haugean tendency very few had university training and many of them had never enjoyed the advantages of higher education in any form. Consequently they were not so enthusiastic for the Norwegian system as were their brethren of the Synod. While they fully recognized the importance of education, both religious and secular, they were not so sure that formal instruction in religious subjects was necessary to the development of Christian character. That was the work of the Spirit and came as a result of the "awakening" and of conversion, which they regarded as a crisis in the spiritual life. A Christian character built on mere human knowledge was likely to remain an unfruitful plant: it was like the fig tree of the sacred story which bore only leaves.

The group that more or less enthusiastically accepted the leadership of Elling Eielsen (and this body was by no means a negligible factor) had never been hostile to the common school. In the "Old Constitution" (which received its final form in 1850) the public-school system was definitely accepted: "The children must be educated in both languages, but in the mother tongue first, though in such a way that the district school is not neglected."[48]

[47] *Skandinaven*, March 19, 1878.
[48] J. M. Rohne, *Norwegian-American Lutheranism up to 1872*, 109 (New York, 1926); J. A. Bergh, *Den norsk lutherske kirkes historie i Amerika*, 30 (Minneapolis, 1914).

" Elling's Friends " can have given but little thought to
the question of parish schools. Their great problem was how
to find, for their vacation schools in religion, teachers who
were known to be converted after their own ideas of what
conversion meant, for a school of religion taught by a world-
ly teacher might prove to be a perilous thing.

In 1870 a new church body was formed under the name of
the Norwegian-Danish Conference. This was to a large
extent made up of pastors and congregations that had earlier
belonged to the Scandinavian Augustana Synod and consequently were of the pietistic tendency. The Conference had
the general left wing attitude toward primary schools; as to
higher education it took a more conservative position, for
the leaders of the Conference believed firmly in the desir-
ability of a carefully educated ministry.

Toward the close of the year 1873 a young theologian
came over the sea to take a professorship at Augsburg Seminary, the educational institution maintained by the Conference. This was Sven Oftedal, and his arrival was a major
event in the history of the Norwegians in the Northwest.
Oftedal was a highly talented man, a strong, energetic leader,
if not a profound thinker. His leadership was daring, confident, and sometimes ruthless, and therefore did not always
attract men to his cause.

After less than a year in his new position Oftedal felt ready
to challenge the Norwegian Synod to defend both its theological system and its attitude toward education. An interview was arranged in which the young professor expressed
a strong belief that all should keep their knowledge of Norwegian bright by daily use. At the same time he stressed
the importance of learning English: "I can only urge in the
most serious terms that all Norwegian children be sent faith-
fully to the public school."[49]

In June, 1877, the subject of primary instruction was discussed in the annual convention of the Conference held that

[40] *Skandinaven,* December 22, 1874. In 1878 Oftedal became a member of
the board of education in Minneapolis; he served in this capacity for ten years.

year in Willmar, Minnesota. M. Falk Gjertsen introduced the subject with a series of theses in the approved way. Gjertsen gave his approval to a system of Sunday schools; where these were impractical he would substitute "everyday schools." In these he would have the Norwegian language used as the vehicle of instruction. Parochial schools organized to teach the subjects ordinarily studied in the common schools he found highly objectionable. In developing this point he formulated a new principle: "No congregation has a right to give instruction in any subject except the Word of God."[50]

This was revolutionary doctrine and could not be acceptable to all his hearers. But, though revolutionary, it was probably not novel. August Weenaas, who as professor of theology had helped to train a large part of the ministry of the Conference, appears to have held analogous views. In a communication sent from Norway in that same year, he declared, "The independence of the Union and the freedom of its citizenship are, under present conditions, contingent upon a serious and successful observance of the principles that lie at the foundation of the American system of education."[51]

Gjertsen's theses were debated but were not put to a vote. Consequently his dictum cannot be taken as the position and policy of the entire convention. Nevertheless, the discussion clearly revealed the fact that this body had a friendly interest in the common school.

VII

Of all the voices that were heard in the controversies of the seventies, the most penetrating was that of Rasmus B. Anderson. Shrill and irritating though it sometimes was, it always had a confident ring; and to his followers (and

[50] *Budstikken,* July 4, 1877.
[51] *Skandinaven,* January 23, 1877; see also the issue of June 5, 1877. Weenaas returned to Norway in 1876 after eight years' service in the schools at Paxton, Illinois; Marshall, Wisconsin; and Minneapolis.

they were legion) the Madison professor seemed to speak ex cathedra. Anderson had sat in silence at the Madison meeting in 1869; he had just lost his position at Albion, and had therefore nothing to say. But only a few weeks later he secured an instructorship at the University of Wisconsin, and his drooping courage revived. He was already beginning to dream of a professorship in Scandinavian languages; six years later his dream was realized (1875).[52]

Shortly after he had entered upon his duties in Madison, Anderson wrote a letter to *Skandinaven* in which he stated his belief that those who look upon the American schools as hostile to religion know very little about them. At the same time the young instructor urged his countrymen to maintain and cultivate their native idiom. " Let us consolidate our influence and accept the American schools; let us labor to the end that our mother tongue may find a place in them. . . ."[53]

This was Anderson's program at the age of twenty-three; he never deviated from it at any subsequent date. At an old settlers' meeting four years later he spoke slightingly, not only of those who found nothing good in the culture of the country to which they had come, but also of the " Norwegian Yankees " who were in too great a hurry to cast aside their ancestral heritage.[54]

During the next few years Anderson took only a small part in the current debates on educational policies. He was giving his energies to the cultivation of older fields, to the Vinland expeditions and to the religion of the Northmen in the Viking Age. Meanwhile the discussion continued with renewed strength. By 1876 the feeling had become exceedingly bitter. The Madison professor was finding it impossible to keep out of the fray.

[52] Anderson, *Life Story*, chapters 26, 30.
[53] *Skandinaven*, October 27, 1869.
[54] *Fædrelandet og emigranten*, July 17, 1873. John A. Johnson spoke on the same occasion and in much the same terms.

Anderson had read a series of articles in *Kirketidende,* the official organ of the Norwegian Synod, in which the public school was condemned on almost every count. He had learned that the church in Decorah had decided to establish a parish school. These developments he regarded as " a declaration of war on the common school." In clarion tones he summoned all Norsemen to rally in support of the national system of education. The common school, he maintained, is the cornerstone of our constitution: " it must and shall be preserved."

Anderson could not be satisfied to remain in a defensive position, however strong; he therefore proceeded to launch a virulent attack on the parochial schools:

Scarcely ever have I seen an American public school so miserable as those pitiful parish schools which the clergy is promoting in the Norwegian settlements. . . . If the Lutheran church cannot exist alongside the common school, then let the Lutheran church perish! And I will say, peace with its ashes.[55]

A few months later he appeared again in print with a caustic attack on B. J. Muus, whose strictures on the public school have been cited above. He showed how inconsistent the leaders of the opposition were in promising to support and maintain an institution to which they imputed such an evil character. He also quoted an ill-considered remark by Professor F. A. Schmidt that " schools where the Word of God is not the ruling power are the gates of hell." [56]

Meanwhile a parochial school had been launched in Anderson's own city of Madison. This was almost more than his sensitive soul could endure. In a bitter communication to his favorite newspaper he expressed the fear that the parochial schools would destroy the common schools. Much as he loved Norwegian he was willing to sacrifice that language, if necessary, to the greater good. Halle Steens-

[55] *Skandinaven,* October 17, 1876; Anderson, *Life Story,* 598.
[56] *Skandinaven,* January 16, 1877.

land, who should have stood by him, received a stern rebuke. The man who had spoken so well in 1871 was now helping to maintain a parochial school.[57]

It must have been some time in this period of the controversy, early in 1877, perhaps, that R. B. Anderson placed the following dictum on his letterhead: " Whosoever directly or indirectly opposes the American common school is an enemy of education, of liberty, of progress. Opposition to the American common school is treason to our country." [58]

Anderson, with Clausen and two others, had staged a dramatic withdrawal from the annual meeting of the Synod in 1868. In the later seventies he was without church affiliations of any sort. But twenty years later he was once more a member of a congregation belonging to the Norwegian Synod. There was much to forgive in Anderson's case, but he was forgiven.

VIII

In the autumn of 1876 a parochial school was opened in Decorah, as noted above. Two teachers were employed, one man and one woman. A church school was also organized in Chicago; in this case the teachers were three: two women and one man. Mention has also been made of a school in Madison. The organ of the Synod noted these developments with natural satisfaction; there was progress at last, even if the actual advance was rather slight.

Anderson's attacks on the church schools were not received in silence. It is to be observed, however, that some of his more prominent critics belonged to the laity. Bernt Askevold, a young teacher and journalist, contributed a series of letters which were, however, of little help to either side. Not much, he seemed to believe, was to be learned in the common school, since the plan comprised " only three or four dry, miserable subjects. . . . On the whole the com-

57 *Skandinaven,* August 21, 1877.
58 Anderson, *Life Story,* 598; cf. *Skandinaven,* March 5, 1878.

mon school is, to my mind, a pernicious school, entirely typical of the national weakness which is peculiar to the American people."[59]

In a second contribution two weeks later he admitted that the common school had its rights but that the parochial school deserved a higher regard. He now seemed to fear that the state might be asked to support parochial schools; this he would not have. Finding that his position was widely misunderstood, he continued in later letters to insist that he really did favor the public school. It was a necessary institution and had a right to the support of all citizens.[60]

C. Lillethun, also a young teacher, who later rose to prominence in Hauge's Synod, looked upon Anderson's activities as warfare against the parochial school. Lillethun said that he favored the common school, but believed that both types might be good. In taking note of the statement frequently made that the common school is the cornerstone of our constitution, he remarked that if the " constitution has no other and better cornerstone . . . it rests, in my opinion, on a weak foundation."[61]

By the later seventies the laity had evidently come to the conclusion that the Norwegian settlements were unable to support two separate systems of education.[62] Nearly all the letters that appeared in the press in those years were friendly to the common school.[63] It was coming to be looked upon as an institution that could bring together all classes, racial elements, and religious groups and teach them the meaning of the great American experiment. Without it chaotic conditions would be sure to prevail. The fact that the common school did not concern itself with religion was

[59] *Skandinaven,* November 21, 1876. Bernt Askevold later entered the ministerial profession.
[60] *Norden,* December 7 and 28, 1876; *Fædrelandet og emigranten,* February 1, May 5, 1877.
[61] *Skandinaven,* November 21, 1876, and April 17, 1877.
[62] *Norden,* January 8 and March 19, 1879; *Skandinaven,* July 3, 1877.
[63] See for example *Skandinaven,* January 2, 9, 16, 30, February 13, 20, 27, March 13, April 3, 17, July 3, 10, and September 4, 1877; *Norden,* March 6 and October 23, 1878, January 8 and June 25, 1879.

held by some writers to be a virtue; others believed that it was not so void of religion as many had feared: our American institutions (and the common school is one of these) are all founded on religion. One contributor affirmed that McGuffey's textbooks were just as good as those prepared by educators in Norway; while another had a good word to say for the American people. In religion, in culture, and in civilization they were, he believed, at least the equals of their Norwegian critics. Prominent, too, was the old argument that the parochial schools were not equipped to give satisfactory instruction in English, a language that all agreed must be thoroughly mastered. It was generally conceded that there was a real need for better teachers in the public schools, and that in the Norwegian settlements these ought to be of the Lutheran faith; but such teachers could not be provided before the church was ready to establish its own training schools and that time would be far in the future.

Among the friends of the American system there were those who hoped that some form of parochial school might be retained wherever economic conditions were favorable.[64] P. P. Iverslie, an incisive and persistent contributor to the Norwegian press, had some such arrangement in mind. With evident reluctance he had come to believe that the pedagogical methods employed in the church schools were inferior and defective. Still, he would not discard these schools entirely. " Let the church school and the common school go hand in hand, each working in its field." [65]

IX

In the spring and summer of 1877 there appeared in *Skandinaven* a series of letters written ostensibly by several persons but more likely the product of a single hand. They were composed in the dialect of Valdres and were addressed

<hr/>

[64] *Skandinaven*, January 27, 1877.
[65] *Budstikken*, November 25 and December 2, 1876; *Norden*, September 24, 1879.

to the immigrants from that region. The author (or authors) pretended to great alarm at the destructive influence of " *Skandinaven*, Professor Anderson, and the Yankee school " and felt that something should be done to remove the peril. The satire was crude and somewhat indelicate; the wit was caustic and cruel; but the satirist was able to sweep into his net nearly all the controverted allegations of his day and the series was thoroughly enjoyed.

The initial letter bore the signature of one Erik i Kroke, whose identity seems not to be known. Erik was much disturbed. A revelation had come to some of the older clergymen that it was sinful to read *Skandinaven;* so he asked his fellow-Valdresmen what had best be done.[66] The outcome was that a Valdres convention was called to meet in Decorah at an early date. Erik i Kroke was asked to preside and after a decent show of reluctance he accepted the honor.[67]

Early in September *Skandinaven* published a report of the Decorah meeting. Evidently the sessions were somewhat boisterous but when Valdresmen were gathered to make war on their enemies one might expect a little excitement. *Skandinaven* was properly denounced; toward the rival *Norden* the meeting was more kindly disposed. Since the common school clearly leads back to paganism (" it puts ideas into the mind of the common man "), it was soundly condemned. The meeting resolved unanimously, " That we establish our own schools to prevent our children from learning anything in the common school."

A committee of three was appointed to deal with Professor Anderson. None of the three being able to write, it was suggested that a young man who had learned to write in the common school be added to the committee. To this there was some objection, since it seemed to involve a dangerous principle: " Education is a good thing in itself

[66] *Skandinaven*, May 8, 1877.
[67] *Skandinaven*, May 26, June 19, July 17, and August 7, 1877.

but a dangerous thing in others." However, since a scribe was needed, the youth was allowed to serve. Among the resolutions reported the following may be quoted:

1. We recognize in Professor Anderson a dangerous principle, to wit education; it is as dangerous as dynamite, since in his case it is combined with keen wit, courage, and a resolute will.

2. We recognize in Professor Anderson a product of the Yankee school and our own stupidity.

4. We lament that he was ever taught writing and arithmetic (the Catechism and the "Explanation" would have been sufficient for that fellow); he is not of the better class. . . .

After adjournment the secretary remained in Decorah for several days to write up the minutes, meanwhile meditating gloomily on the progress of evil in a wicked world.[68]

After the close of the decade of the seventies little is heard of parochial schools. It is not likely that the common school was in serious danger at any time during the years of the great controversy. The expense of a dual system of education and the lack of efficient teachers were considerations that could not be brushed aside. There was a growing conviction that American citizenship implied a loyal support of the common school. Important, too, is the fact that in the early years of the eighties a violent controversy broke out in the Synod, one that led to a serious defection a few years later. The new conflict consumed all the energy available for propaganda and in the circumstances the cause of parochial education could no longer be promoted with any hopes of success.

[68] *Skandinaven*, September 4, 1877.

My earliest memories go back to a little Norwegian community in northern Iowa where my family had located a year or so after we had come from across the sea. I recall the time when our settlement counted only a single dwelling, which was, moreover, a dugout. But soon houses rose on neighboring farms; the boundaries of our community moved forward to meet those of the older communities farther east; and in time our locality was merged with many others into one of the largest Norwegian settlements in the Northwest. That, however, was some years later; in my boyhood we were still in the stage of little things.

In those lonely days in the earlier seventies the appearance of a stranger among us was almost an event. A traveler was always welcome and was invited to share such comforts as we had; but if by chance he spoke our own language the welcome would be doubly cordial. Among the more interesting strangers who came to the settlement were certain persons whom the farmers called "laymen." These might be oldish men with whitened hair, like Hans Tønnesen Steene, who looked in upon us in his old age; or they might be young men, like Stener M. Stenby, who was still in the earlier twenties when he visited our locality. Mostly, however, they were men of middle age who had labored in the vineyard many years not only in this country but also in the old home.

In most respects these visiting laymen resembled the farmers whom we saw from day to day. Their hands were calloused and discolored. Their faces looked as if they had never had a close acquaintance with the edge of a razor; nor was it likely that professional barbers had ever touched their heads. They moved about with a heavy stride like men who had long known the meaning of unremitting toil.

Sometimes the visitor would go out into the farmyard or the field to assist his host with his daily task, and it was soon made clear that his hand had not lost its cunning. But the labor was often retarded as much as it was promoted; for the visitor liked to talk, and he could not long refrain from this delightful occupation.

Though I did not know at first what a layman was supposed to be, it was not long before a few things were made quite clear: he was evidently some sort of preacher, for he spoke at "meetings" very much like the clergyman who came to the settlement at rare intervals. Sometimes the farmers appeared to think that his sermons were better than those of the regular minister. He was much more energetic and spoke with the confidence of a prophet. He laid the sinner on the anvil and gave him blow after blow. At the same time he had neither the manner nor the appearance of a priest. He wore inexpensive clothes, not much better than those of our neighbors, while the clergyman wore a long black coat that looked both rich and expensive. Moreover, he spoke with no attempt at correct syntax, and the peculiarities of his speech were often so clear-cut that his hearers could very nearly determine the region or the valley from which he had emigrated.

It was explained to me that a lay preacher was one who had not been trained for the work of the priesthood, had not been called to serve a specific congregation, and was therefore not ordained to the work of the divine ministry. But that did not mean that his activities were regarded as in any sense irregular; far from it. The advocates of lay activity believed firmly that a layman might have a valid call to labor for the promotion of the kingdom, as valid as any call that was signed by church officials. This call came from the spirit and there was, therefore, a lay ministry which some would regard as equal in holiness to that of the regular ministry. Nor would they admit that these preachers were ill informed. Though they might not have mastered all the futile and often pernicious learning of this seductive world, in all those matters that concerned salvation and all its tremendous implications they were thoroughly informed and should be heard with respect.

Scoffers might object that the lay preacher had only one sermon in his repertoire and the charge was frequently true. No matter what scripture was used to introduce the discourse, his actual text was likely to be the cry of Saint John in the wilderness, "Repent ye, for the kingdom of heaven is at hand." At all times the emphatic word was "repent." His great task, as the preacher saw it, was to awaken souls who were asleep in sin; and this he believed could not be achieved through historical and theological disquisitions. Such matters could be left to those who wore the black gown and the white ruff. As for himself he would go on in the old way calling souls to repentance.

Nearly all the preachers who came to my father's house professed the Lutheran faith; and while some of them had certain theological eccentricities, in all essentials they were honestly faithful to the Reformation standards. However, we occasionally heard preachers, both lay and ordained, who belonged to what our leaders called "the sects." There was a strong Methodist congregation of Danes and Norwegians at the county seat, a society of sufficient means to build the first church in the town, perhaps the first in the county. At one time this church had a dozen or more lay preachers who no doubt proved quite helpful in seeking out and bringing in those who might have Methodist proclivities. The Baptists were also active and gathered a considerable number of Swedes, with a few Norwegians, into a church just outside the town. Then came the Adventists and again the waters were stirred. A strange individual who professed to be a Quaker went in and out among us for many years. The burden of his preaching was that the children of God are not under the law, but they naturally do what is right in the sight of the Lord, no matter what the laws of this blind world have to say about it.

In all this there was nothing unusual. Our community was simply passing through a stage of religious chaos that was common in frontier settlements. The religious life of the pioneer was much disturbed (and sometimes diverted) by the clash of discordant opinions. The claims put forth by those who preached antinomianism, Arminianism, perfectibility, adult immersion, the observance of the seventh day, the imminent end of the world, and the annihilation of the wicked had, of course, to be fairly considered with a view to successful refutation. Social calls tended to become so many hours with the Bible. The Book was brought forth; relevant texts were read and discussed. Sometimes highly irrelevant passages were also brought into the debate and defended as vigorously as were those that were clearly pertinent.

In this Babel of discordant voices the voice of the Lutheran lay preacher could easily be distinguished above all the others; for he came with an old message that all had heard in earlier days, one that all could readily understand. He was not an organizer and formed no churches; but he led disturbed souls out of their mental confusion and back to the old faith. He taught the essentials of a system into which the thinking of the Norwegian pioneer could naturally fit itself. For what he brought was not novel in any sense; it was what all Norwegians had once learned from the Catechism and the " Explanation."

II

Though all the lay preachers were (or believed themselves to be) Lutheran in doctrine and Haugeans in their attitude toward life, some of them were charged, and often quite truthfully, with un-Lutheran practice, in that they employed the methods of their Reformed rivals. This criticism was not seriously received, however, by those who believed that lay activity had Biblical sanction. Furthermore, it seemed inevitable that there would be borrowing of this sort; nor would such borrowing be necessarily wicked. It was during the seventies that Dwight L. Moody and his lesser associate, Ira D. Sankey, acquired their great fame as evangelistic workers. The conservatives might shake their heads and grumble that such methods were entirely foreign to Norwegian church life; but they found it very difficult to pronounce unqualified condemnation on the work of these remarkable men.

Our own itinerants, who usually traveled on foot or in lumber wagons and carried no musical instruments, could have no vocalist companions; but that did not deter them from venturing to imitate the methods of the famous preachers. Some of them harbored an odd conviction that they could sing, and sing they did. And it may as well be admitted that their audiences often found the song acceptable and even edifying.

Hans Bodelsen, who conducted a series of meetings in a schoolhouse near our home, was unlike the average layman. Having had the advantage of city life, he had become acquainted with urban ways and had appropriated the finer things in urban culture. There was a polish to his manners which contrasted vividly with the rural bluntness of his fellow preachers. His language was also more in accord with accepted standards. On the other hand, he had the usual Haugean mannerism, a monotonous intonation of a somewhat lugubrious character which many of us found decidedly unpleasant, but which others regarded as quite natural to a " spiritual " discourse.

After the close of his sermon Bodelsen would begin to sing. His hymns were sung to melodies of the lighter sort, though he took great care to use no tunes that might be regarded as lacking in dignity. A melody that he often used was the one that had become associated with the well known song, "Long, Long Ago." He also employed the expedient of the after-meeting. When he had preached and sung, he would begin to address us a second time. This discourse was more informal than the first; it was delivered in a sitting position and in a more natural voice. There were those who grumbled about this part of the service; one sermon in an evening ought to be sufficient. Nevertheless, the audience always remained till the last hymn had been sung.

Bodelsen also had literary interests of a sort. He had collected a group of short stories with a distinctly religious content which he had published under the title *From Darkness to Light*. He had also written an account of his own career, which had not been without a real variety of experiences both pleasant and unpleasant. Lay preachers often had books to sell, but they were usually not of their own composition. When one finds an exception to this rule, one also finds that what was called a book was scarcely more than a pamphlet.

Stener M. Stenby came a few years later. The farmers liked the appearance of the youthful evangelist with the serious, almost ascetic countenance. Bodelsen's message had been warm and hopeful; was he not himself " a brand plucked from the fire " ? Stenby was inclined to be more judicial and severe. He, too, undertook the role of the soloist. His favorite hymn was a Swedish song set to a melancholy tune of haunting beauty. It was an appeal to cast aside the frivolities of the world " for the eyes of God are upon you and vengeance is dogging your steps." The farmers loved to hear the song, for the preacher sang effectively; but one may be allowed to doubt the wisdom of closing a service on the note of divine vengeance.

All our preachers were not itinerants. Some of the more effective workers limited their activities for the most part to their own locality; only rarely did they go into the wider held. On a Sunday one of these would be ready to lead in divine service, if his neighbors wished him to do so. Usually the meeting would be held in a schoolhouse, though in the winter a private home might be found more convenient. A hymn would be sung, prayer would be offered, and the leader would proceed with what he would call " a few remarks." If he thought it wiser to do so, he, or one of the others present, would read a sermon from a *postil.* In my own community two such collections were popular: one by Ludvig Hofacker, a German preacher of great power, and another by Lars Linderoth, a Swedish divine whose unsparing denunciation of his own degenerate times was always heard with cordial approbation. Meetings of this sort were never held, however, when there were religious services elsewhere in the neighborhood, even if these were of a sectarian character.

The head of our household was such a preacher. He was priest in his own house; he was the religious leader of a considerable part of the community. He looked upon his duties on Sunday as something that the local situation seemed to demand. A clergyman came to visit us eight or ten times a year; but this provision was scarcely adequate for the needs of the community. When the church services became more frequent and regular, these informal gatherings were discontinued.

III

For several decades a violent controversy raged all the way across the pioneer settlements on the subject of lay activity. The Norwegian Synod believed that such activity, unless regulated by the church authorities, was to be condemned. The leaders of the Synod found that it was contrary to the teachings of the Augsburg Confession and therefore could not be approved. If a layman wished to preach they would have him present himself before the authorities of an orthodox church body, asking to be examined. If the examiners were satisfied, he might be given a license to preach. It is possible that some were actually licensed in this way, but on this point the writer has no information.

To the lay preachers and their adherents this was a most unreasonable demand. It was clear that their opponents were giving the Confession an incorrect interpretation. Then, too, the authors of that famous document may have been mistaken on some points. But whatever the Confession said, the lay preachers were convinced that it was not only their right but their Christian duty to prophesy. In support of this belief they were able to quote a goodly number of passages from Holy Writ. So lay activity continued.

For more than half a century the history of the Norwegian church in America was the history of two traditions which were more or less at variance with each other. The one was that of the state church with its emphasis on an orderly church life and on the sacred functions of the ministerial office. This tradition was represented by the Synod; it was the force that gave to that great church body its characteristic tendency and direction. The opponents of the Synod charged its ministry with an ambition to rebuild the church establishment of the homeland on Western soil. No doubt this was true in part, for there was much in the ecclesiastical system of that country which the leaders in Wisconsin and Illinois regarded as worth transplanting. But to reproduce the Norwegian system of church government cannot have been seriously considered.

The second was the Haugean tradition. The Haugeans were never cordial in their general attitude toward the official clergy. Even some of the symbols of the old order were offensive to them, and they hoped that in the western settlements they would see nothing of them. They objected strenuously to such externals as the ministerial gown and the white ruff, "the millstone" that the state had hung about the neck of the priesthood. These were badges of an authority that had sometimes proved quite oppressive to delicate consciences; they were therefore not seen with pleasure.

The Haugeans also objected to the ease by which men could become members of the local church. In Norway the churches had to be inclusive, but in the free states of the West it should be possible to have a selected membership. Some wished, accordingly, to have a definite assurance that the applicant was converted or at least "awakened." Others were anxious not to draw the lines too narrowly, seeing that hearts are not so easily searched. All were in perfect agreement, however, that men who obviously lived in sin should never be admitted to the fellowship of saints.

Both the Haugeans and the conservatives were to discover that overseas ideals and practices could not be maintained on American soil without serious modification. So long as the Haugeans were an informal body existing within an inclusive establishment, they could maintain their rigid exclusiveness; but now that they were forced to become an organized body, it was not easy to carry on in the old way.

Similarly, the conservative element, which from the outset had clung to the ideal of a thoroughly educated ministry, found to its dismay that this ideal could not be entirely realized. Norwegian graduates in theology were not keen about emigrating, and the number of trained men who presented themselves for ordination with a view to work in the American fields was wholly inadequate to meet the demands of an expanding population. The Norwegian Synod therefore found it expedient at times to consecrate candidates whose training was far below the standard that the church sought to maintain.

It is a startling and also a highly significant fact that for more than twenty years such divine services as the Norwegian pioneers were privileged to attend were conducted chiefly by laymen, or by laymen who had received ordination. And in saying this I am not forgetful of the fact that J. W. C. Dietrichson worked in the Koshkonong area a part of that time; but the sloop folk had been in America nineteen years before Dietrichson came, and he remained only five years, all told. During this period he labored energetically and organized several congregations. Unfortunately Dietrichson was by temperament a high churchman, and the pioneers were not ready for such a system as he tried to establish among them.

The earliest lay preacher of whom there is record is Ole Olson Hetletvedt, who came in the "sloop" in 1825. The history of Norwegian church life in America properly begins with his activities. Hetletvedt had been a schoolmaster and was probably the best educated man in the group. He began his work as a preacher in the Kendall settlement in western New York but later transferred his activities to the Fox River country in northern Illinois, to which many of the Kendall settlers moved in 1834 and the following years.

Another of those early lay preachers was Bjørn Hatlestad, who came west in 1836 or perhaps a year or two later. Ole Heier, a young "reader" from southern Norway, came in 1837. Heier was a very effective speaker but seems to have been lacking somewhat in intellectual stability. Soon after his arrival he was attracted to Mormonism, but after a brief stay with the Latter-Day Saints he began to look for another fold and closed his career as a preacher in the Baptist church.

Rasmus B. Anderson in his *First Chapter of Norwegian Immigration* gives a list of seventeen preachers who were active in the first decade of our history.[1] All but one of

[1] Page 431. The list reads as follows: Ole O. Hetletvedt, Bjørn Hatlestad, Ole Heier, Gudmund Haugaas, Knud Pederson, Hans Valder, Jørgen Pederson, Elling Eielsen, Claus L. Clausen, J. W. C. Dietrichson, Even Heg, Endre Osmundson Aaragerbø, Herman Osmundson Aaragerbø, Kleng Skaar, Aslak Aae, Peder Asbjørnson Mehus, and John Brakestad. Three of these, Eielsen, Clausen, and Mehus, were ultimately ordained to the Lutheran ministry. Jørgen Pederson and Gudmund Haugaas along with Ole Heier joined the church of the Latter-Day Saints.

these were laymen, or began their careers as lay preachers. It may safely be assumed that the sixteen were all of the Haugean tendency or adhered to that movement. Since the Norwegian communities were as yet neither large nor numerous, one may conclude that they did not suffer from a dearth of preaching. And when one adds to the Lutheran contingent a group of missionaries who represented the Reformed churches, the number of spiritual advisers, especially in the Fox River Valley, becomes abnormally large.

IV

Into the religious chaos that ruled in the Fox River settlement there entered in 1839 a crude but insistent force which in a few years brought at least a semblance of order to the distracted community. The new force was the virile preaching of Elling Eielsen, the most famous of all the Norwegian lay preachers in the New World.

Eielsen was a native of Voss. In the year when he came to Illinois he was thirty-five years old. He was a man of strength, of experience, and of unshakable convictions. A decade earlier he had entered upon the career of an itinerant preacher and as such had traveled over large parts of Norway. In 1837 he had extended his activities to Denmark where he ran afoul of an old law forbidding religious conventicles and was cast into prison. This was an experience which gave him great satisfaction: now he, too, had been permitted to suffer indignities for preaching the Word of God.

That the young preacher was endowed with a forceful personality cannot very well be denied; but in some of the finer graces that distinguish successful leadership he was sadly wanting. He never learned how to travel comfortably on the highways of compromise and made little effort to come into agreement with his adversaries. His opponents (and they were many) made much of Eielsen's narrow Haugean view of life, of his stubborn willfulness, and of his deep aversion to the externals of official churchliness; and one is soon convinced that these attributes were prominent in his character. But one must remember that two traditions, two theories of what a church is and ought to be, were in conflict in the little settlements in Illinois and Wisconsin, and that in this controversy Eielsen's opponents were as unwilling to seek accommodation or compromise as he ever was. On all sides the demand was the same, "They must come into agreement with us."

But with all his shortcomings Eielsen was able to form close friendships and to inspire unwavering loyalty among those who shared his point of view. It is therefore quite proper that his following should come to be generally known not by its official name, the Evangelical Lutheran Church in America, but simply as Ellingians, Eielsen's Synod, or more often as "Elling's Friends." Rarely in our history has a personality stamped itself so indelibly on those with whom it came into friendly and intimate contact.

There was work to do in the settlement, and Eielsen proceeded to the task with characteristic energy. In powerful tones he called on his countrymen to abandon the "sects" and return to the Lutheran fold. He built a house, of which the upper story was used for religious gatherings under his leadership. Even if this building was not a consecrated church, it has a prominent place in the history of religious life in pioneer times. The outcome of Eielsen's activities was that a distinctly Lutheran element began to take form. The sectarians were routed, all except the Mormons, who retained a following in the Fox River area for several decades.

Eielsen soon extended his labors to the settlements of southern Wisconsin; and as new centers of population were formed, his field of activities widened correspondingly. He was a typical circuit rider, only he usually did not ride. Equipped with knapsack, ax, and coffee pot he traveled on foot from settlement to settlement. Wherever he found a group of homes where his own language was spoken, he was sure to tarry to offer the consolations of the divine Word.

There was one need in these communities that neither Eielsen nor his fellow workers could supply: this was the need of sacramental observances. Marriages could be performed by justices of the peace, though bridal couples much preferred the blessing of a clergyman. (The writer has known faithful Lutherans to go to the Methodist minister for the wedding ceremony rather than be " squired.") In an emergency, baptism could be performed by any Christian, and religious life in pioneer times was almost a continuous emergency. Funerals could be managed by the men of the settlement, who often served as ministers, sextons, and undertakers on the same occasion. But how were the children to be confirmed? And who had authority to administer the Lord's Supper? For it was Haugean doctrine that these rites were necessary and that both were the peculiar function of the priesthood.

Even before Eielsen had come to Fox River, no doubt in 1837 or 1838, steps had been taken in the settlement to form some sort of a religious organization. Jørgen Pederson had been chosen to the leadership with authority to administer holy communion. There is record of at least one occasion when Pederson served in this office; however, he soon abandoned his flock and joined the Latter-Day Saints.

Eielsen cannot have been long in Illinois before his new friends approached him with the request that he seek ordination. One has a right to believe that he was reluctant to take this step; but he could not help feeling that after eighteen years without the services of a regular pastor, his compatriots surely had a good right to ask for such an official. Accordingly he appealed to a German Lutheran clergyman in Chicago, Francis A. Hoffman, by whom he was consecrated according to Lutheran rites on Sunday, October 3, 1843.

For many years there was doubt as to the legality of this

ordination: it was a rule in the church that a candidate seeking this rite must be properly called and examined, and Eielsen had no formal call and did not submit to examination. One must remember, however, that there was probably no one in authority in all the land who could examine Eielsen. That in his four years in the New World he had become somewhat acquainted with the English language cannot be doubted; but that his knowledge was adequate for a theological test is quite unlikely. An emergency existed and it was dealt with in the best possible way.

Two weeks later C. L. Clausen was ordained, also by a German clergyman. Clausen was educationally better prepared than Eielsen, but he, too, was without the usual theological training, and up to the time of his ordination must be classed among the lay preachers. The two new pastors found it impossible to work together and Clausen soon found more congenial colleagues in a group of young ministers educated at the University of Christiania who began to arrive in Wisconsin in the later forties.

For a number of years Eielsen was the one and only pastor to a large Haugean element scattered throughout the Norwegian settlements. Most of this following was in Wisconsin and Illinois and in the adjacent parts of Iowa and Minnesota; but the great traveler at one time even thought it necessary to visit isolated groups as far away as Missouri and Texas. Associated with him was Endre Johannesen, who begins to appear in the records in 1847; but Johannesen seems to have been definitely located in the Fox River area. Eielsen was pastor at large; his parish was wherever Norwegians lived and could be assembled in house or church. Meantime, he depended on a group of lay preachers to keep the fires burning on the altars of Haugeanism, each in his own locality.

Among those who may be regarded as of this group were Paul Anderson, Ole Andrewson, and Andreas A. Scheie. Anderson was not a typical lay preacher, but the other two fall readily into that category. Anderson had been awakened by the preaching of Hetletvedt; Scheie was one of Eielsen's own converts. All three sought and received ordination at the hands of American Lutheran church authorities. Whether they inconsiderately deserted their chief or were repelled by his eccentricities is a moot question; at any rate they parted company with him and took a line that led eventually to the founding of the Augustana Synod.

Much the same happened a decade later when P. A. Rasmussen withdrew from the Eielsen connection. Rasmussen came to America in 1850 as a young man of twenty-one and was soon to acquire wide fame for the eloquence of his preaching. Seeing the need for specific training, he entered a German seminary at Fort Wayne. He was ordained by German clergymen. He returned from Fort Wayne with a somewhat modified point of view, and, though for two years he labored actively in Eielsen's church, he could not always see eye to eye with his chief. In 1856 he withdrew from the Haugean fellowship. Ultimately he accepted membership in the Norwegian Synod.

V

At the annual meeting of the Haugean churches in 1854 Eielsen brought up the question of pastoral help. Congregations had now been formed in several states and the call for ministerial service was insistent everywhere. At the time there were three ordained men in the Haugean connection: Eielsen, Johannesen, and Rasmussen. The last two, having parishes in the Fox River country, could be of no great help to Eielsen outside Illinois; but it was clearly impossible for one man to cover an area that now extended from Lake Michigan all the way westward into Iowa and Minnesota.

Gudmund Strand, a prominent layman from Koshkonong, "thought that in order to relieve the present need persons might be used who possess a Christian temperament and sound conception of the truth, even if they do not have the education which one could otherwise wish or regard as necessary." This view found general approval and Torbjørn Tjentland was warmly recommended for ordination. The nominee declined, however, on the plea of failing health.

Eielsen had been an ordained pastor and the recognized leader in his church for nearly fifteen years before he was ready to ordain anyone to the holy office. The first to be set apart in this way were Arne Boyum and Gudmund Strand, both of whom received ordination in 1858. Strand was a man of sixty-four years with a long record as a preacher on both sides of the sea. Five years earlier he had been requested by Haugeans in Norway to visit America with a view to learning why there was so much contention among the brethren in Wisconsin and Illinois. Strand remained in America. It is clear that he was a man of more than ordinary abilities. During Eielsen's absence in Europe in 1861–63, he was the acting president of the church.

In the nineteen years from 1858 to 1876, inclusive, Eielsen and his associates ordained twenty-four men, all of whom had served an apprenticeship as lay preachers.[2] In age they ranged from twenty-five to sixty-four; Arne Boyum and Østen Hanson were the youngest and Gudmund Strand was the oldest. Several were in the neighborhood of fifty years. Three only were below thirty. This means that nearly all were seasoned men and experienced preachers. It also means that in many cases the years of the pastorate would be few and that the church would be in a constant need of active ministers.

[2] The following list includes the names of all these men with the year of ordination: 1858, Arne Boyum and Gudmund Strand; 1859, Lars Johnson (Amundsrud); 1861, Østen Hanson; 1863, Peter Thompson (Sandve); 1864, Ole E. Torgerson; 1866, P. L. Solberg; 1868, Ole A. Bergh and Hans E. Sether; 1869, Fredrick Herman Carlson and Ole J. Kasa; 1870, Jens A. Höiland and Lars O. Rustad; 1871, Gunder L. Graven; 1872, Herman William Abelson, Johannes Halvorson, and Rasmus O. Hill; 1873, Staale Berntzen, Christoffer O. Brøhaugh, and Markus Sampson; 1874, Ingvald Eisteinsen; 1875, Lars L. Eittrem and Andreas Nelson; 1876, Anfin O. Utheim. In addition to these twenty-four, Eielsen's church ordained two men who had been trained in theological seminaries: Andreas P. Aaserød and John Zach. Torgerson. It is to be noted that these two did not remain many years in the fellowship.

Among these twenty-four a few had served as teachers and doubtless had received a certain measure of professional training. One or two had given some attention to higher studies, though the time spent in this way cannot have been long. But the great majority of Eielsen's colleagues were wholly without training, as the world understands the term. They were carpenters and shoemakers, sailors and farmers, who believed that they had heard the call of the spirit and had gone forth to preach in response to this call.

One is not to conclude from this, however, that these men were inferior personalities or inefficient pastors. Perhaps they could not shine on the higher levels of theological debate; but for the work that most of them found to do they were peculiarly well equipped. Among them, too, were men who were endowed with the qualities of leadership: there is no discounting the importance of churchmen like Arne Boyum, Gudmund Strand, Østen Hanson, and Rasmus Hill. A few like Christoffer O. Brøhaugh and O. A. Bergh had literary interests which they indulged as their duties allowed. The men who gathered about the chieftain from Voss may have been lacking somewhat in culture and refinement, but they were not wanting in intellectual strength.

In 1876 Eielsen's organization made important changes in its constitution and modified the name to Hauge's Synod for the Evangelical Lutheran Church. The "Old Constitution" was Eielsen's own work and it was very dear to him. Though he bitterly resented the changes, he was at first disposed to acquiesce, for he was reluctant to part with his old associates. A dissenting element, however, brought strong pressure to bear on the aging man and he finally took his place as the leader of this remnant. Only one minister, Peter Thompson, remained with him in the older fellowship. At the time of the division Eielsen was seventy-two and Thompson sixty-one years old.

There was real fear among Elling's Friends that their organization might not survive the passing of the two leaders.

Eielsen was therefore strongly urged to ordain additional pastors. It was made clear to him that, if for any reason he should be unable or unwilling to act at the ceremony of consecration, his colleague would be asked to serve in his stead. Eielsen yielded and in 1881 he ordained two lay preachers, Mons Langeteig and Ingebrigt Johnson. The new ministers were both elderly and of the same age, sixty-one years. Less than two years later the old chieftain passed away.

Since 1881 there have been several ordinations in Eielsen's Synod and most of those set apart have been lay preachers, but not all. For some time the church has had its Bible school where most of the candidates for the ministry have spent a period of preparation for pastoral duties. Some of the pastors have also studied at other institutions. It is not to be inferred from this, however, that the ministry among Elling's Friends has become conventionalized; for the old belief that a season of lay preaching is the best apprenticeship for those who aspire to the priestly office is still held in its old vigor.

VI

When Paul Anderson and Ole Andrewson took leave of the Eielsen connection they first associated themselves in a loose way with the Franckean Synod of New York, from the ministry of which Anderson received ordination in 1848. Three years later they helped to organize the Northern Illinois Synod, a body which was American, German, and Scandinavian in its membership. After nine years in this affiliation the Swedes and Norwegians withdrew and formed the Scandinavian Augustana Synod. This body continued Scandinavian till 1870 when the two nationalities separated and two Augustana Synods came into being, one of which, the Swedish, has flourished mightily to this day.

The ministry of the Northern Illinois Synod felt no compunctions about consecrating laymen if they seemed to be qualified for pastoral work. Of the nine Norwegians who received ordination from, or were licensed by, this organization, five were lay preachers.[3] The youngest of these was Ole J. Hatlestad (a nephew of the lay preacher Bjørn Hatlestad), who was thirty-one years old; the oldest was Nils Olsen (Fjeld), who had ten years more to his credit. The policy of the Synod was, however, to encourage those who had ministerial ambitions to take some time for theological study. To achieve this purpose a "university" was established in Springfield, Illinois, at which several Norwegian students received such training as was thought necessary in those days for successful ministerial work.

In the Scandinavian Augustana Synod an identical policy was pursued. Johan Hveding and Johan Peter Gjertsen, ordained at the ages of forty-five and sixty-two respectively, had both enjoyed educational advantages far beyond those of the average lay preacher, but neither seems to have had any specific training in theology. Seventeen other Norwegians received consecration from the same ministry; but in every case the candidate could show credentials from some theological institution, though in most cases the training received could have been neither extensive nor thorough.

After the division of the Augustana Synod, and in the same year, the major part of the Norwegian group, with the co-operation of certain elements from the outside, organized a new body, the Norwegian-Danish Conference. Meanwhile the minority kept the old name and was for two decades known as the Norwegian Augustana Synod. This reorganization produced no change in policy in the matter of lay activity. Lay preaching was approved and encouraged; and while the ministry preferred to ordain only such men as were formally trained in theology, its membership was not averse to consecrating laymen if they seemed to possess the neces-

[3] These were Ole J. Hatlestad, Ole Anfinsen, Peder L. Asbjørnsen (Mehus), Nils Olsen (Fjeld), and Osmund Scheldahl. Hatlestad states (*Historiske meddelelser*, 56) that Ole Andrewson was ordained by this same body; but Andrewson was apparently performing ministerial duties as early as 1846, or five years before the Northern Illinois Synod was organized. See *Who's Who among Pastors*, 28.

sary qualifications.   In the fifteen years following the organization of the Synod five such men were set apart for
service at the altar, all of whom were known as pulpit orators
of more than usual power and effectiveness.[4]

Of all the lay preachers that the writer has been privileged
to hear, the most gifted was Knud Salvesen.   Salvesen owed
nothing to the schools; a few days of attendance in a primary
school was all that he had to his credit.   But he had read
much and had thought much, and in this way had stored
his mind with much of what is best in human culture.   As
a sailor he had seen a great deal of the world, and he had
sailed for many years.   His preaching was simple, direct,
forceful, and eloquent and his audience seemed never to tire,
though the sermon might sometimes go on past the hour.
It was inevitable that a man of such positive talents should
be brought into the regular ministry.   He received ordination at the age of sixty.

When Eielsen separated from his old associates in Hauge's
Synod, the mantle of leadership fell upon the shoulders of
Arne Boyum.   Three years later the new theological school
in Red Wing was in active operation, and in the years that
followed the church recruited its ministry quite largely from
the successive graduating classes of this institution.   But
Hauge's Synod also continued the earlier practice of ordaining laymen: by 1917 nearly a dozen lay preachers had been
received into the ministry.   The last candidate from this
class was apparently Jonas B. Falkanger, who received ordination in 1910.[5]

[4] Andreas Wright, a Minnesota farmer, was ordained in 1870. Ole E.
Hofstad was admitted to the ministry in 1873. Knud Salvesen, sometime sailor
and farmer, received ordination five years later. There were no further ordinations of lay preachers until 1885, when acceptable candidates were found in
two recent immigrants, Knut Christian Hinderlie and Carl Julius Olsen.

[5] The roll reads as follows: 1877, Iver Tellefsen and Markus Nielsen; 1878,
Bersvend Anderson, H. Hendrickson, and Anders O. Oppegaard; 1885, Gøran
Norbeck; 1888, Johannes L. Kyllingstad; 1895, Kittel T. Strand; 1903, Jens H.
Johanson; 1907, Ole H. Haugen; 1910, Jonas B. Falkanger. It is possible that
the list is not entirely complete, since in a few cases sufficient information is not
at the writer's disposal.

VII

When the decade of the seventies came to its close, there were four organized church bodies in the Northwest which claimed the loyalty of those who wished to maintain the Haugean tradition. On the extreme left were Elling's Friends, while the Conference occupied a strong position on the right. The other two synods, Hauge's and Augustana, held more central positions. The careers of these two bodies illustrate the power of the presumably dead past. Though in agreement on all essentials, they found it impossible to unite because of various things that had happened in the years gone by.

Toward the question of lay activity the attitude of these four bodies was almost identical. All made use of such talents as were found among the laity, though lay activity was probably under more positive control in the Conference than in the other three churches. Theoretically, too, they all favored the elevation of gifted lay preachers to the ministerial office; in practice, however, there was some difference. Theological seminaries had now been established by all the Norwegian church bodies except Eielsen's Synod and emphasis was everywhere placed on a trained ministry. And so it came about that after the close of the seventies the practice of ordaining lay preachers became quite unusual, except, of course, among Elling's Friends.

So far as the writer is able to learn the Conference admitted no laymen to the ministry. Lay preachers might be ordained, but only after a period spent in theological studies. The Lutheran Free Church, which may be regarded as having inherited the traditions of the Conference, has deviated from this policy, but only in rare instances.[6] The Lutheran Brotherhood has ordained at least one lay preacher.[7] The policy of the Norwegian Synod has been much the same as that

[6] Such lay preachers were Morris Eggen (1923) and Peter Overlid (1920); perhaps also Jacob Samuelsen (1903).
[7] Halvor L. Westel (1899).

of the Conference. Lay preachers have been consecrated by that body but only after a time spent in some approved theological seminary or after a rigid examination by synodical authorities.

During the eighty years from 1843 to 1923, the various churches ordained 68 men who seem clearly to belong in the category of the lay preacher. In addition to these I find sixteen pastors whose status is not so easily determined; they seem to be men with more training than the average lay preacher had received, though they all doubtless served in the same apprenticeship. This brings the total up to 84. One must also remember that a considerable number of such preachers enrolled in seminaries and received consecration, not as laymen but as theological candidates. The writer has made no attempt to sort these out, but if their number is added to that given above, the total is sure to go far beyond the hundred mark.

Nor must we overlook the fact that among the lay preachers there were many who never aspired to the ministerial dignity. They were content to go on with their work in the old irregular and untrammeled way. Some of them achieved very little, but the achievement of the group taken as a whole must have been quite significant. And when these are brought into line with those that are numbered above, they become a large company, an important unit in the discordant and factious army that was doing battle for the old faith.

As one looks back over our history one is amazed at the great controversy that lay activity kindled in the Norwegian settlements. One might think that there would be a keener realization of the vastness of the field and the paucity of qualified workers. It is not necessary to elaborate what has been said above as to the significance of lay activity; but one may at least say this, that what Eielsen did for his countrymen and his church in the Fox River Valley, lesser men did in lesser communities all over the Northwest.

There can be no doubt that the activities of these preachers were often destructive. They brought turmoil to settled communities and rent congregations into contending churches or factions. On the whole, however, their work was constructive. They built crudely at times and often they exaggerated the feature of bald simplicity; all the same, they built.

Lay preaching was something that belonged to the frontier. It flourished because there was a need that such preaching, conditions being as they were, alone could satisfy. It showed its greatest strength in the decade of the seventies. In that decade the frontier was moving swiftly westward toward the arid lands. By 1890 frontier conditions had in a large degree disappeared. With more settled conditions in society came more settled conditions in the church. The growth of higher educational institutions in secular life was paralleled on the religious side by the building of theological seminaries. The time had come when trained men could be sent out into the newer settlements, and the favor in which lay preaching had once been held suffered a progressive decline.

With the passing of the frontier one notes a corresponding decline in certain forms of individualism. The pioneer was an incorrigible individualist, and the Haugean preachers shared generously in the same belief. There is a great deal to say for the passionate self-reliance that characterized the men who built the civilization of the West; but as usual there is also another side to the shield. Exaggerated individualism is sure to breed contention and to give birth to faction, with unfriendly division as the inevitable result. If it should seem necessary to prove this assertion, the proofs will be found in great abundance in the history of the Norwegian-American churches.

One sometimes wonders what might have happened if

those who cherished the Haugean tradition could have organized themselves into a single unit and could have maintained that organization through the trying decades of pioneer times. No doubt our history in such a case would have had a far different development. It is even possible that such a body would have drawn to itself a greater strength than that which came to its less contentious opponents. But it is useless to speculate on what might have been; the duties of the historian are concerned with things as they actually were.

INDEX

INDEX

For the convenience of users the characters _æ_ and _ø_ are alphabetical respectively as _ae_ and _o_.

Abbott, Ezra, 91
Academic professions, Norwegians in, 27–36
Accountancy, 28
Adventists, 149
Against Heavy Odds, 107
Ager, Waldemar, author, 54
Agersborg, H. P. K., zoologist, 30
Albany Medical College (Albany, N.Y.), 30
Albion Academy, 127, 140
Aliens, in America, 8–13, 68, 71. _See also_ Americanization
America, 10, 11, 52, 87, 94, 102, 154, 156, 161, 162
"America Book," 49
America Not Discovered by Columbus, 22, 52
Americanization, 14, 41, 79, 89, 103, 124
Americans, native, 4-6, 10, 11, 39–41, 47, 67, 68, 80, 144
Andersen, Arthur, 28
Andersen, Hans Christian, 96, 108
Anderson, Andrew Runni, 31
Anderson, Arthur von Krogh, 30
Anderson, John, 123
Anderson, John August, 32
Anderson, Paul, 160, 164
Anderson, Rasmus Bjørn, pioneer author, 22, 24, 51, 156; academic career, 52, 127, 140; leader in student uprising at Luther College, 126; organizes education society, 126; champion of the common school system, 127, 139-143, 145
Anderson, William, 28
Andrewson, Ole, 160, 164, 165n
Anthony, Susan B., 89
Anundsen, Brynild, 53
Arne, 58
Askevold, Bernt, author and journalist, 52, 54, 56, 60, 66; criticizes the common school, 142
Astronomy, 28, 32
Athens, American school in, 31
Atlantic Monthly, 51, 92, 97, 98, 99
Augsburg Confession, 153, 154
Augsburg Seminary, 24, 138

Augustana Synod, the Norwegian, 165, 167
Augustana Synod, the Scandinavian, 128, 138, 161, 164
Austria, German, 10

Bacteriology, 30
Baptists, 7, 149, 156
Barnard, F. A. P., 95
Bassoe, Peter, 29
Beder, S., 88, 89
Beloit College, 127
Benson Grove (Iowa), 39, 44, 45
Berdahl, A. J., 132
Berdahl, Clarence A., 31
Bergeim, Olaf, 29
Bergh, Ole A., 162n, 163
Bevins, Frank, 45
Bevins, James, 45
Bevins, William, 45
Bierman, Adolph, 77
Biology, 30
Bjørnson, Bjørnstjerne, author and politician, 58–60, 93, 107; influence 58–60, 61, 66, 99, 101; visits Northwest, 105
Blegen, Carl W., 31
Blegen, Theodore C., 32, 49n, 58n
Bodelsen, Hans, 151
Boone, Daniel, 9
Boraas, Julius, 27
Boston, 90n, 91, 93, 102n
Botany, 28, 30, 34
Boyesen, Alf, 90n
Boyesen, Algernon, 112, 113
Boyesen, Austa, 83n, 111n
Boyesen, Bayard, 112, 113
Boyesen, Hjalmar Hjorth, author and poet, 22, 50–52, 60, 66, 82–85, 91, 92, 97–109, 112, ancestry and early life, 83–87; emigrates to America, 86–88; journalist, 50, 88, 89, 95; tutor and professor of languages and literature, 51, 90, 92, 96; influenced by Bjørnson and Turgenev, 59, 60, 99–101; religious affiliations, 88, 93, 111; champion of the common school, 89; hostile toward Norwegian clergy, 103–105; interest in German